The Real Experts:
Readings for Parents of Autistic Children

Edited by Michelle Sutton

Owned by disabled workers, Autonomous Press
seeks to revolutionize academic access.

Autonomous Press is an independent publisher focusing on works about disability, neurodivergence, and the various ways they can intersect with other aspects of identity and lived experience.

ISBN-10: 0986183563

ISBN-13: 978-0-9861835-6-0

Cover art by Alyssa Hillary. Yes, the same one that's in this book. Go read sier essays. Or order art from **Because Patterns** (https://www.facebook.com/BecausePatterns).

Table of Contents

Foreword

This book is for parents of autistic children.

It's also for grandparents, aunts and uncles, and other relatives—not to mention teachers, therapists, support staff, and anyone else involved in the care and upbringing of a young autistic person. This book will also be of value to scholars and researchers studying autism, and to academic faculty like myself who are involved in training the next generation of professionals in fields like psychology and education. But first and foremost, Michelle Sutton put this book together with her fellow parents in mind.

Every good and loving parent in the world faces the same question every day: *How do I help my child to thrive?*

Every time a truly good and loving parent makes any sort of parenting choice, however big or small—whether it's choosing a school or choosing a bedtime story, choosing when to put a toddler down for a nap or choosing what rules and advice to give a teen about dating— that is the question we must answer as best we can, the question that guides our decisions, even if we never put it into words.

How do I help my child to thrive?

Any good parent can tell you that this question is endlessly challenging. No matter how many times we grapple with it and find what we hope is a good answer, a new situation is guaranteed to come along soon that requires us to grapple with it yet again and to find yet another answer. And sometimes we have to wait months or years or even decades to find out how good our answers were.

If your child is autistic, and you're not autistic yourself, the question of how to help your child to thrive becomes a hundred times harder. But this is *not* because being autistic is in any way incompatible with thriving. Rest assured that autistic people *can* thrive, and do thrive. Autistic people, including your child, can have good lives full of joy and love and meaningful connection and creative fulfillment.

So why *is* it so hard to determine how to help your autistic child to thrive? Most of the difficulty can be traced to three factors.

The first factor is that your child's sensory experience of the world is fundamentally different from yours, and the way your child's mind works is fundamentally different from yours. So different that it may be nigh-impossible for you to imagine what your child experiences, senses, thinks, knows, or feels, or what your child is trying to communicate, or why your child is doing some particular thing. And this, of course, can make it quite difficult to figure out what your child needs. Fortunately, the insights of autistic adults can be of great help in this regard. Autistic adults have been there. They have insider knowledge.

The second factor is that there's so much misinformation and bad advice about autism out there. Many of the standard "expert" or "professional" approaches to autism are badly misguided and rooted in ignorance. For instance, there are certain "therapies" that are widely recommended for autistic children but that are actually harmful and traumatizing (the most widespread of these, Applied Behavior Analysis or ABA, is addressed in some of the writings in this book). When so many of the "experts" are so utterly wrong and so confident in their prejudices and misinformation, it's hard to know who to listen to. Here, again, the insights and insider knowledge of autistic adults are invaluable.

The third factor is that because the minds, interests, experiences, abilities, and needs of autistic people are different from those of non-autistic people, "thriving" also looks different in autistic people than it does in non-autistic people. Health, happiness, success, personal fulfillment, good relationships, psychological well-being, a high quality of life—all of these things are possible for autistic people, including your child, but the autistic versions of these things are often quite different from the non-autistic versions.

When you're trying to help a "typical" child to thrive, the society in which you live provides you with many models of what a thriving child looks like, and many models of successful, thriving adultood. These models provide some idea of what you're aiming for, some idea of what you want to help your child to become. But parents rarely have access to models of what a thriving *autistic* child looks like, or a successful, thriving autistic adult. So how do you know if your autistic child is on the right track, developmentally, when the "right track" for your child might be vastly different from the established societal standards of what the "right track" looks like?

Most non-autistic "experts" are unhelpful about this sort of thing, because they regard autism as intrinsically unhealthy, intrinsically a "wrong track." Most non-autistic "experts" think that key to helping an autistic person thrive is to try to make them non-autistic, or to try to make them as "indistinguishable" from a non-autistic person as possible. Making an autistic person into a non-autistic person simply can't be done (though sadly, many parents fall prey to unscrupulous quacks and cultish organizations selling phony and expensive "treatments" for autism). And trying to make an autistic person outwardly "indistinguishable" from a non-autistic person ultimately does the autistic person far more harm than good, as you'll see in some of the personal accounts in this book.

So when it comes to the question of what the path to a good life might look like for your autistic child, autistic adults can yet again offer crucial insight, and can also serve as inspiring examples.

Michelle Sutton, who put this book together, is the mother of six children, two of whom are autistic. Listening to the insights and experiences of autistic adults has helped Michelle to help her autistic children to thrive.

The dozen autistic people who have contributed their writings to this book (and I'm honored to be one of them) are all thriving, in our own ways. Most of us had a hard time getting to the point where we were thriving, and many of us are still recovering from the hard times we had. We accepted Michelle's invitation to contribute to this book because we want the next generation of autistic children, including your child, to have an easier time. Like you, we want your child to thrive.

Nick Walker
Berkeley, California, 2015

❖ ❖ ❖

Introduction

This is the first time my name has appeared on a book. I'm really not sure if I've done it "right," but, like most things in life, I've approached it with the attitude that if it feels important I should probably do it. This felt important, simply because all the people I'm going introduce you to in the pages of this book are people who have helped me immeasurably in my journey as a parent to Autistic kids.

You know, there are so many blogs and books written by parents of Autistic children (I have a blog or two myself), and that's okay, but when it comes down to it the Real Experts on autism are Autistic people themselves. So it makes sense to me that the people I should be listening to when I need insight about autism are Autistic people.

I've been fortunate to have the opportunity to know and talk to many amazing Autistics, and I feel honoured that those in this book have agreed to let me publish their words. As I spoke to them about this project and how it would best work, I realised that what I would end up with is a collection of some of my favourite blog articles by Autistic authors. These articles are my favourites for various reasons, and they speak in different styles about a variety of issues, but all have been important in my parenting growth.

I know that not all voices appeal to all people, but I feel confident that in the pages of this book there is something for every parent of Autistic kids. Some of what is written here you might want to hear, some of it you might need to hear. Some of it will have a big impact on you now, some of it might become more relevant to your life a couple of years from now. Some of it will make you feel reassured, some if it will really make you think.

So, with my unending gratitude and thanks to all my Expert friends in this book, and to the wonderful team at Autonomous Press, here is the collection of essays by Autistic people that I think every parent of Autistic children should read. I hope you find it helpful.

Michelle

❖ ❖ ❖

Nick Walker

Nick Walker is an Autistic educator, author, speaker, transdisciplinary scholar, parent, and martial artist, and a founding editor at Autonomous Press. He holds a 6th degree black belt in aikido, and is founder and senior instructor of the Aikido Shusekai dojo in Berkeley, California. He is a faculty member in the Interdisciplinary Studies program at California Institute of Integral Studies and the undergraduate Psychology program at Sofia University, and also a longtime member of the experimental physical theatre group Paratheatrical Research. Nick is a leading thinker in the emergent field of neurodiversity, and has been deeply involved in Autistic community and culture since 2003.

I met Nick online in a group for bloggers writing about Autism. When I read Nick's writing I immediately recognised that he was talking about the kind of attitude toward Autism and acceptance that I want my kids to experience. Through his blog, *Neurocosmopolitanism*[1], Nick introduced me to the word **neurodiversity**, and has helped me understand how crucial to my children's wellbeing it is that I speak out about the dangers of pathologising Autism.

Each of the two articles Nick has graciously agreed to let me publish in this book brought me to turning points in my journey as a parent.

The first, "What is Autism?", is the single best explanation of Autism I have ever read. I recommend it to every parent of a newly diagnosed child I speak to, both online and in "real life."

The second, "This is Autism," is a beautiful and intimate glimpse

---

1.   URL: http://neurocosmopolitanism.com

into how Nick lives his life as an Autistic person. It is real, honest, and full of positivity and hope.

Both the articles can be found on Nick's blog, which I cannot recommend highly enough.

What is Autism?

Nick Walker

Autism is a genetically-based human neurological variant. The complex set of interrelated characteristics that distinguish autistic neurology from non-autistic neurology is not yet fully understood, but current evidence indicates that the central distinction is that autistic brains are characterized by particularly high levels of synaptic connectivity and responsiveness. This tends to make the autistic individual's subjective experience more intense and chaotic than that of non-autistic individuals: on both the sensorimotor and cognitive levels, the autistic mind tends to register more information, and the impact of each bit of information tends to be both stronger and less predictable.

Autism is a developmental phenomenon, meaning that it begins *in utero* and has a pervasive influence on development, on multiple levels, throughout the lifespan. Autism produces distinctive, atypical ways of thinking, moving, interaction, and sensory and cognitive processing. One analogy that has often been made is that autistic individuals have a different neurological "operating system" than non-autistic individuals.

According to current estimates, somewhere between one percent and two percent of the world's population is autistic. While the number of individuals diagnosed as autistic has increased continually over the past few decades, evidence suggests that this increase in diagnosis is the result of increased public and professional awareness, rather than an actual increase in the prevalence of autism.

Despite underlying neurological commonalities, autistic individuals are vastly different from one another. Some autistic individuals exhibit exceptional cognitive talents. However, in the context of a society designed around the sensory, cognitive, developmental, and social needs of non-autistic individuals, autistic individuals are almost always disabled to some degree—sometimes quite obviously, and sometimes more subtly.

The realm of social interaction is one context in which autistic individuals tend to consistently be disabled. An autistic child's sensory experience of the world is more intense and chaotic than that of a non-autistic child, and the ongoing task of navigating and integrating that experience thus occupies more of the autistic child's attention and energy. This means the autistic child has less attention and energy available to focus on the subtleties of social interaction. Difficulty meeting the social expectations of non-autistics often results in social rejection, which further compounds social difficulties and impedes social development. For this reason, autism has been frequently misconstrued as being essentially a set of "social and communication deficits," by those who are unaware that the social challenges faced by autistic individuals are just by-products of the intense and chaotic nature of autistic sensory and cognitive experience.

Autism is still widely regarded as a "disorder," but this view has been challenged in recent years by proponents of the neurodiversity model, which holds that autism and other neurocognitive variants are simply part of the natural spectrum of human biodiversity, like variations in ethnicity or sexual orientation (which have also been pathologized in the past). Ultimately, to describe autism as a disorder represents a value judgment rather than a scientific fact.

❖ ❖ ❖

This is Autism
Nick Walker

Old Cutter John comes to town, leaving Las Vegas before dawn and driving across desert and mountains to Berkeley nonstop, no sleep, fuelled by coffee and chocolate and a whole lot of CDs full of music to play over and over again with the volume on the stereo of the rental car turned up to eleven.

The CDs are mix CDs he made, and mix CDs I made for him. For a few years we shared an obsession with making these mix CDs and sharing them with one another and with friends. Each CD is a collection of songs we like, united by a particular theme, or a complex set of interrelated themes. They are musical stories or treatises; soundtracks to unmade movies about whatever aspects of life we were contemplating at the time. The themes are not simple, it's not like, "This one is a collection of my favorite love songs, and this one is a dance mix for parties." Titles of our various mix CDs include *The Mark of Cain*, *100 Years of Solitude*, *Where They Never Have Troubles*, and *The Logistic Difference Equation*.

Like me, Old Cutter John is an Autistic activist. He's also my father. I recently discovered that many people in the Autistic activism community—including people who have been friends with both Old Cutter John and I for years—were unaware that he was my father. We've never tried to conceal the fact from anyone. It just never occurs to us to mention it if no one asks.

Once Old Cutter John mentioned to someone that he's known me for decades. The person asked where Old Cutter John and I had first met.

Old Cutter John replied, "In a hospital."

This is autism.

It's a bright cool Sunday in Berkeley, and when I step into my aikido dojo the sun is singing through the skylights, suffusing the big airy space and making shiny hot pools of white on the rich vibrant blue of the mat. That vibrant expanse of blue makes a low soft thrumming and gives me a feeling of warm wide open spaces behind me and in the lower part of my lungs. The sunlight sounds like a choir of angels, and together with the pleasantly humming mint-flavored whiteness of walls it makes my skin tingle and opens a luminous sky in my chest and all around my head. I inhale into that space and the cool air fills my head with exhilarating white-blue and brings new, higher harmonies into the choir.

There's a moment of silence waiting for me at the top of the inhale, and just as I reach it I realize that another sound is happening, too, a grey-brown sound that rolls and tumbles like an otter in the blue-white river of sensation. This sound is incongruous and merits investigation, so as I begin to breathe out I do that trick that I learned to do when I was a real tiny kid, the trick that no one ever talked about and that I could never explain to anyone because, as I eventually learned long after I grew up, for most people it's not a trick that they have to do, it's just the way they are all the time. The trick where I filter and sort and separate the currents of the river until they resolve themselves into a world of discrete objects with names and meanings.

Dojo, walls, blue mat on blonde wood floor. Seven of my aikido students in white gi, early arrivals for class, on the mat, stretching. The choir is still singing blue-white, the walls still have that minty tingle. Interpreting some of the currents and eddies of the river as discrete objects with names doesn't make the river stop. The flow is always happening. The world of discrete objects and names is a part of the river, too, and it's the part where most other people live by default. Me, I'm just visiting.

Once I've made the necessary shift in consciousness, it becomes clear to me that the grey-brown tumbling otter sound that got my attention was someone talking to me. A greeting, I think, from one of the students on the mat. Yes, he's looking at me.

Quick mental checklist, made quicker by the fact that I don't think in words and thus don't have to go through it in a linear fashion. If it were a literal checklist, though, written out in words, it would go something like this:

Does his greeting call for a response on my part?
Yes, definitely.

Is he smiling?
Yes.

Should I smile back?
Yes.

Do I already happen to be smiling?
Yes. How convenient!

Does this exchange of greetings also require speech on my part?
Most likely.

Have I now taken so long to respond that there may be some potential social awkwardness to navigate?
Probably not. In terms of clock time it's only been a few seconds. A slightly longer pause than is usual for the ordinary rhythms of social conversation, but my students are quite accustomed to my pauses by now.

"Good Morning," I say, smiling.

I bow, because I'm entering the dojo, and one bows when one enters the dojo.

It's past noon by the clock, but I say *Good Morning* because I always say *Good Morning.* Yet another quirk to which my students are well accustomed.

I like to remember that it's always morning *somewhere.*

This is autism.

Julia and Zoe come to town. We meet on the porch of a Thai restaurant near my apartment in North Berkeley. Julia is taller than I expected. It is my intention to have Thai food for lunch, but Julia has not experienced Thai food and is reluctant to do so at this time.

There was a long period in my adolescence and young adulthood when I would have regarded Julia's reluctance to eat Thai food as something that I should help her to overcome, by badgering her in the manner that I learned as a child from Sam I Am in Dr. Seuss' *Green Eggs and Ham.* "Would you eat them in a box? Would you eat them with a fox?"

Now, though, my years of immersion in the emergent Autistic culture have deeply inculcated in me a rule that I think of as the Golden Rule of Neurodiversity: *Respect the bodily, sensory, and cognitive needs of others as you would want your own to be respected, whether or not you understand the reasons for those needs.*

So I suggest an establishment across the street, that serves good cuisine of a more Euro-American variety. A place where Julia and Zoe can have pancakes with whipped cream for lunch, while I can have a large salad with grilled chicken and some sort of spicy ginger dressing that satisfies my own sensory preferences. The noise and bad acoustics inside this establishment are unpleasant for all three of us, so we elect to sit at a table out on the sidewalk. Julia has found a small purplish flower somewhere, and she twirls, twirls, twirls it between her thumb and forefinger while we wait for our food. We all watch the flower, watch it spin, spin, spin.

This is autism.

Kassiane comes to town. We lunch on delicious Thai food, on the porch of a Thai restaurant near my apartment in North Berkeley.

I've been reading Kassiane's activist writings online for more than a dozen years. Her writing is fiery and powerful, the writing of someone who has learned well and truly that the consequences of standing up and pushing back hard against the forces of oppression are never as bad as the consequences of *not* pushing back. I know a lot of people who are scared of her. I regard her as a hero.

In person, Kassiane is smaller that I expected, and she has a white cat named Purkinje who rides on her shoulder. She looks ten years younger than her age, and her voice is soft and light, easy on the ears. She loves the color purple. I've seen photos of her with purple hair, but today it's brown. She might or might not be wearing purple. I can't tell. It doesn't matter. Because everything she does is a beautiful bright purple. My brain processes her voice as purple, her movements as purple. She's warm and friendly, and when she hugs me, she means it, and I feel like I've been enveloped by a purple glow.

This is autism.

When my daughter was born, I suspected from very early on that she wasn't Autistic. I didn't mourn, not even for a moment, that my daughter's neurocognitive orientation was different from my own.

When non-Autistic parents have Autistic kids, this is what I wish for them: I wish that they would accept their Autistic kids as Autistic, and instead of trying to raise them to be like non-Autistic kids, raise them as Autistics and help them to grow into the best Autistic human beings they can be.

So when I had a non-Autistic kid, I decided to practice the Golden Rule, accept her as non-Autistic, and raise her to be the best non-Autistic human being she could be.

Non-Autistics do all this fascinating complex social stuff—but how do they learn to do it? I immersed myself in the study of developmental psychology, and set about making myself an expert on non-Autistic childhood development. How much eye contact do non-Autistic kids need? What's the best way to help them develop spoken language and non-verbal communication skills? What do they need in order to feel safe and socially confident?

When we're immersed in projects that are meaningful to us, there's no folks as thorough as us Autistic folks. I did such a thorough job of helping my daughter achieve her developmental potential as a non-Autistic kid that she ended up with social and communication skills that were advanced far beyond the usual norms for non-Autistic children her age—and with social confidence to match. Now I have to figure out how to deal with having a child who can charm most people into giving her anything she wants.

This is autism.

Lydia and Shain come to town. Lydia is speaking at UC Berkeley, and they're staying in a hotel near campus. We make plans to meet for dinner in the evening, after they return from a day across the Bay in San Francisco.

They're headed back into Berkeley on the BART train—the local commuter rail system—and I'm walking to meet them. All through the walk, I'm getting rapid-fire text messages from Lydia, with updates on their progress, questions, refinements in the evening's plan. Can I meet them at the BART station instead of at the restaurant? Sure. Is there room in my car for them? I don't have a car and I couldn't drive one if I had it, but I can meet them on foot and walk with them to the restaurant via the shortcut through UC Berkeley campus that I'd been planning to take.

I am a great admirer of both Lydia and Shain. They are two of the most important Autistic activist voices of their generation. I'm in awe of Lydia's writing—not just its quality and its importance to Autistic activism, but also how prolific she is.

This conversation via text, while I'm walking to meet them, is a reminder of Lydia's prolific writing output: she is apparently capable of texting faster than I can usually talk.

When they arrive, I discover that in conversation, Lydia talks like she texts. Not just the sheer speed of it, but also the style. She uses abbreviations in speech that I'm used to only seeing in text messages or Facebook status updates: OMG, FML. I quickly discover that the only way I can process her speech is by picturing her statements typed out in my head as text messages.

Throughout the evening, interspersed with her conversation with me, Lydia initiates brief, spontaneous side conversations with Shain, in which she shares thoughts that have suddenly occurred to her, concerning characters in her unpublished novels or characters in roleplaying games—thoughts that Shain has the necessary background information to appreciate, while I don't. It occurs to me that outside of Autistic culture, some people might find this rude. I don't find it rude at all. I find them both to be charming company, and these side conversations strike me as delightful glimpses of the intimate connections these two share, sort of a verbal equivalent of the affectionate, aikido-infused physical play in which my wife and I so frequently engage in public.

First order of business, before we can head across campus to the restaurant, is to find a bathroom. It's a busy warm night in Downtown Berkeley, and the sidewalks of the main streets are bustling with people.

Me, I love the sensory experience of navigating a busy nighttime sidewalk: all those different bodies moving in their own ways, with their own paces, rhythms, and trajectories. Finding the spaces between them is a dance much like the dance of aikido.

But just as I'm about to lead my guests into a particularly busy stretch of sidewalk, I remember the Golden Rule of Neurodiversity: *Respect the bodily, sensory, and cognitive needs of others as you would want your own to be respected, whether or not you understand the reasons for those needs.* And I remember that the pleasure I find in this particular form of sensory stimulation is a relative rarity among Autistics. So I quickly ask them whether they prefer crowded sidewalks or quiet ones, and Lydia tells me they'd prefer quiet, and I do a swift detour down the nearest quieter street.

We have delicious Ethiopian food for dinner. I walk them back to their hotel, which *does* involve crowded sidewalks: the boisterous stretch of Telegraph Avenue near campus, which on warm nights like this is teeming with drunken students, local youth, and homeless folks of all ages. A lot of the homeless folks who hang out on Telegraph Avenue have dogs, and Lydia and Shain stop to make friends with every single dog we pass.

This is autism.

Riki comes to town. She knows the species, traits, and potential uses of every plant in the neighborhood. She smells of patchouli and walks with a cane, and my daughter loves her.

Riki spends hours fixing my out-of-commission electric scooter, taking it apart and putting it back together. It seems to me that she's doing me a great favor working on my scooter, but from Riki's perspective, I'm doing *her* a favor because she's never had the opportunity to take this sort of scooter apart before. The whole time she works on the scooter, she talks to it like she's a friendly veterinarian talking to an animal. She refuses to take a break to eat.

Afterward, I take her out for Thai food.

This is autism.

The youngest and most enthusiastic student in my aikido dojo, the girl is five years old and so small that even the smallest size of gi is adorably large on her.

She *loves* aikido. Like me, when I started my own aikido training at the age of twelve, she has a hard time learning the moves, but she keeps on working at it because she gets what the art is about, she appreciates its sublime beauty in a way that most people, so far as I can tell, don't arrive at until they've been training for ten or twenty or thirty years.

That's my secret, really. The secret to how I got to be a sixth degree black belt in aikido, and the chief instructor of a thriving aikido dojo. Most people assume that I had some sort of natural physical talent for it, but nothing could be further from the truth. The secret was that the beauty of the art touched me, that I could see from the beginning that its dance contained all the sublime subtle grace that I saw and loved in the flight of birds and the movement of the ocean's waves. And even though I had no talent for the art at all, I wanted so much to feel what it was like to embody that grace, that I was willing to put in as much work as I had to in order to get there.

More than three decades later, I'm still at it; I've gotten far enough now that I've had some first tastes of that grace, now and then in recent years, and it's just served to whet my appetite.

This little girl can see the beauty, too. And today, before class starts, she can barely wait to talk to me. But she still remembers to stop and bow when she enters the dojo. The Autistic kids always remember.

After her bow, she comes bounding across the mat to me.

"Hello, Sensei," she says.

"Good Morning," I say.

"Today is a special class!" She informs me, looking somewhere past my left shoulder. "Today is my fifty-third aikido class!"

"Ah," I say. I think for just a moment, then it comes to me. "That's a prime, isn't it?"

"Yes!" she laughs, and bounds away across the blue mat, hands flapping.

❖ ❖ ❖

Ally Grace

Ally is an autistic woman. She lives with her autistic partner and their four autistic children, in Australia. They are an unschooling, no punishment family, with dreams to travel around the country. Ally strongly believes in challenging the pathology paradigm of autism. She blogs about her family, about rejecting conventional autism assumptions, challenging social norms around raising children, unschooling, and being autistic at suburbanautistics.blogspot.com.

Ally's blog, Suburban Autistics, is refreshing in its candour. Ally's direct style of writing is thought-provoking and without guile, gently reminding readers of the importance of kindness and respect in the parent-child relationship.

I chose this piece, "Letter to an Autism Mama," because it is the perfect antidote to the feelings of hopelessness and fear it is easy to find in too many parent-written blogs. It is the letter I would have loved to read when my daughter was first diagnosed. Ally knows the struggles and gently encourages us to look deeper, to look for more than what the "experts" and professionals would have us see. This piece is a must-read for all parents of Autistic children.

Letter to an Autism Mama

Ally Grace

Dear Autism Mama.

Beautiful Mama. Tired Mama. Worrying Mama. Brilliant Mama.

Are you feeling scared right now?

Your perfect little child, born with ten fingers, ten toes, and soft skin that melted your heart; that child who grew to crawl and walk and love and smile; is that child suddenly seeming not so perfect?

Have you spent evenings crying about your mothering, worrying that you just aren't cut out for this job?

Have you spent evenings thinking about your child, wondering what his future holds for him?

If so, then I want to reach out and take your hand. I want to give you a smile and a hug. And I want to tell you that it is all going to be okay.

If you are feeling numb, I want to tell you that the sunshine, and the clouds, and cappuccinos with marshmallows on the top, and stars up in the night sky, and autumn leaves falling to the ground in a splendour of orange, and waves lapping on the white shore of the beach, and rain dripping down the windows, and flowers in bloom, and especially your love for your child... I want to tell you that all of those things will help you to be happy. I want to tell you to just love your child. Nothing could be easier, surely.

I want to watch your child and tell you that he is beautiful and perfect. I want to say hello to your child and not expect him to answer me. I want to give your child a gift and not expect him to say "Thank you." I want to tell you how adorable your child is. I want to watch your child line up his toys, and smile with you over a coffee about his quirks and passions. I want to listen to you tell me about his amazing memory, his attention to detail, the things you just know he understands, and his favourite video.

And I want to tell you what I know about autism.

Autism is something that your child is born with, deep in his genetic coding. It is a way of life and a way of being. Your child is autistic, and autism is a part of every single thing that your child ever does. Autism is neurology. It is not a disease, your child is not sick. Your child does not need to "get better." Your child is not "brain damaged." He is autistic, now and forever. You cannot wish your child's autism away. You cannot wish away something that is such an integral part of a person, without also wishing away that unique person whom you love.

I want to tell you that the "experts" don't know what it feels like to be autistic. That the "experts" used to believe that autism was caused by "Refrigerator Mothers." The "experts" used to believe that all autistic children needed to be institutionalised. That electrocution was a good "treatment" for autism. That autistic people had no feelings or emotions. Some of the "experts" *still* believe such things.

And now those same "experts" are telling you that there is something "wrong" with your child. That autistic people are "damaged." That autistic children are "burdens" and "dangers" and "tragedies." That autistic children have no chance of living a happy life in this world. And maybe those experts are telling you what to do about that.

Maybe they are telling you that your child needs an IQ test. Maybe your child has already had an IQ test and has not tested "well." Maybe they are telling you that your child needs to start "therapy" or "treatment" as soon as possible. Maybe they are telling you not to expect too much from your child. Maybe they are telling you that your child is never going to live a "normal" or meaningful life. Maybe they are telling you that your kindness is wasted on your child. Maybe they are telling you that your child is manipulative, stubborn and rude. Maybe they are telling you that autism is not "curable" and that you child will be "afflicted" for life. Maybe they are telling you that your child is "low-functioning"; maybe they are telling you that your child is "high functioning." Maybe they are telling you that all this love you have given your child is wrong, because your child needs "tough love," therapy, and strict enforcement of "consequences." Maybe they are telling you that your child only understands "black and white", and that there is no point in ever trying to speak to, or reason with, your child.

Whatever it is that they are telling you, it is probably misguided, ignorant, insensitive, and damaging.

And a core thing that is missing from this "expert" knowledge is an understanding of which "autistic symptoms" are innate, and which ones are caused by the way we have historically treated autistic people.

Autistic people have complex souls. Autistic people need to be loved, unconditionally, wholly, and with abandon. Autistic people need relationships—especially with you, their mother. Autistic people have favourite things, favourite toys, and favourite people. Autistic people like to play, laugh, sing, and enjoy life. Autistic people will work with what they have been given by their parents and by their home environment.

But maybe the most important thing I want to tell you is this:

As all people travel through life, so do autistic people.

Being autistic isn't being at a train station, it's being on a train.

Your child will grow over his lifetime.

Your child will surprise you, make you proud, make you smile, and make you thankful.

Your child will grow, learn, change, morph, and develop.

Your child is holding inside of himself, amazing things. If you are lucky, you might get to see some of those things.

Your child has potential that maybe you cannot see right now.

But just because you can't see it, it doesn't mean that it isn't there.

If at any time you see darkness, or feel that you are lost, look harder. Look harder and wider and with different eyes, and find the joy in your life. Find the joy in your child. Find the love and remember the journey. Remember that this is not the station. Autism is something that you have to learn to understand with time; it is a journey for you as a parent, a learning journey. Trust the journey.

I have four children who are autistic.

My children will never lead a "normal" life. I speak to, laugh with, and reason with, my children. My children are not manipulative. My children are not "naughty," My children do not think in "black and white," any more than other children do. My children are sweet and caring. My children experience deep feeling, and have special ways of expressing themselves. My children do not need "tough love." My children need me. And my children need love and acceptance.

My children bring me great joy. My life is not perfect, nor constantly joyous. But I can see gifts in my children, I can see their souls and their faces and their smiles. I can see that they are perfect little people. They are them, and I do not wish for more than that.

It is up to me to equip myself to be the best mama I can be, the best carer for them. This is what will give them the best chance they have for success and happiness in life, wherever they may find those things.

My children do not always speak well, but they are learning.

My children fight, but they are growing wiser.

My children scream and stomp and rage, but they also reflect in their own quiet way.

My children, like all children, are going through this rite of passage that we call childhood. And I have been honoured with this job of caring for them. I have amazing children, and I will take my children into adulthood with all the spirit and the wisdom that I can muster.

I will never stop seeing my children as worthy, as capable, as responsible, as lovable, and as perfect people in their own right. I will never stop celebrating my children for precisely who they are.

20 years ago, I was an autistic child. I was the child who was "naughty," who always did the wrong thing, who thought Santa was not going to leave me any presents, who was yelled at and hurt and sent to my bedroom without any dinner, who didn't have friends, who kicked and screamed and scratched and cried and who felt miserable and alone. I was the child who was bullied and didn't know it. I was the child who didn't understand the world I was living in. I was the child who wrote stories but didn't play. I was the child who didn't eat because the food was smelly and made me gag. I was the child that none of the other parents wanted to have over. I was the child who didn't smile. I was the child who didn't get invited to birthday parties.

And today, I am an autistic adult. I look back and I see that I was not given the right assistance, the right parenting, the right explanations, the right level of patience, the empathy I needed, the right words, or the right reactions. When I grew up, I was thrust into the world far too early. I wasn't ready and I suffered for it. A few years on from that, I don't always make the right choices but I am always growing. I work hard and I am learning every day. I think I am worthy of love, and I think that I deserve happiness and success in life. I was not accepted by my family or by the society of which I am a part. But I accept myself because I am valuable. And I accept my children because they are valuable.

So, dear mama. Please love your child. Hold your child close. Cuddle them whenever they will let you, and certainly whenever they seek out a cuddle. Throw out their uneaten food without despairing.

Listen to their voices and their bodies and their eyes and their hands. Wait for those words and those cuddles and those times that you cannot predict. Don't believe it when those well-intentioned but ignorant men and women with University degrees tell you that your child is a no-hoper.

Don't give up on your parenting dreams. Cling on to the dreams of pancakes in the morning, cuddles at night, sunsets on the porch, and teddy bears tucked under blankets.

Cling on to the dream that you would have a beautiful child to love and to raise.

Because, perfect Mama, you do.

Emily Paige Ballou

Emily Paige Ballou grew up near Kansas City, Missouri, and attended the University of Georgia, graduating with degrees in both biology and drama. She currently lives in New York City, where she works as a stage manager for new plays, new musicals, and the WordPlay Shakespeare series. She also serves as a volunteer for the Autism Women's Network, and as co-moderator of the blog We Are Like Your Child. *She has been previously published on the* NeuroQueer *blog and in the online literary magazine* Barking Sycamores. *She drinks probably too much coffee, and misses walking in the woods.*

Emily's blog, *Chavisory's Notebook*[1], is a treasure trove of her stories about her life. It is sometimes informal, sometimes quite academic. It is always worth a look as Emily speaks candidly about her life.

On the blog Emily has a page of quotes. One of them strikes me as relevant to this book:

> *"You change for two reasons: Either you learn enough that you want to, or you've been hurt enough that you have to."*
> - Unknown

Emily's blog has been part of my journey of learning that has lead to change in the way I parent. The article I share with you here, "You Should Tell Your Kids That They're Autistic," was first published in 2013 and is an excellent explanation of the importance of knowing your identity. I have shared it often since I first read it.

---

1. URL: http://chavisory.wordpress.com

You Should Tell Your Kids That They're Autistic

Emily Paige Ballou

"How hard it is to say what it was like
in the thick of thickets in a wood so dense and gnarled
the very thought of it renews my panic.
It is bitter almost as death itself is bitter.
But to rehearse the good it also brought me,
I will speak about the other things I saw there."

- Dante's *Inferno*

I've seen this passage quoted before by others in order to explain what it's like to grow up autistic and not knowing. It's still by far the best explanation of that feeling I've ever read.

For Autistics Speaking Day this year, I want to say something unequivocally. And it's incredibly rare that I feel qualified to just tell other people what they should do, but—if you are an autism parent—

Please tell your kids that they're autistic.

Or have autism. Or Asperger's Syndrome. Or are on the spectrum. Whatever. They can make their own choices about language preference later.

I don't know your kid, so I don't know when the right time or the right age is, or whether the best way is to have a talk and tell them all at once; or slowly, in trickles of information over time; or to simply always talk about it at home so they grow up always knowing.

However you tell them, just tell them the truth. It's worth it.

1. They already know that they're different. You can't keep them from knowing they're different by not telling them.

I knew when I was 3 years old. I could tell things were harder for me than they were for other kids. I could tell when I didn't understand things that other people did (and when they couldn't understand things that I did), I could tell that other people didn't have as hard of a time explaining what they needed and getting it, that I didn't know what I was supposed to do when other people expected me to, that I was expected to know things I'd never been told. That I didn't know how to dress, that I didn't get invited to parties. That things hurt my ears, that being touched felt wrong, that I was ignored by every single girl in my 5th grade class except one for the entire year.

We have very good pattern recognition. It's very hard not to notice, actually, when every single description of the world you're given… doesn't quite match up with your perception.

And being told by adults that I was wrong, that I was imagining it, didn't make me wrong about what was happening; it made me not trust adults.

2. They deserve to know. They are entitled to accurate information about themselves.

If you had a kid who was gay or transgender, would you want or expect them to go the rest of their lives without the self-knowledge and self-acceptance involved in claiming those labels? Or without the ability to seek out information, history, appropriate health care, emotional support, and community with others if they wanted it? Why should those things be denied to an autistic kid?

(I wrote that and then realized that of course there are parents who would deny those things to an LGBTQ child. But I hope you wouldn't.)

That someone is autistic is information about their brain, about their body, about their life, and they are the rightful owners of that information.

Most people I know who either found out their diagnosis, or received a correct diagnosis as a teenager or adult, were relieved to have the knowledge, but resentful of their parents having kept it from them. I know people who are glad not to have been diagnosed as a child—mostly because of the awful things it was considered acceptable to do to autistic kids when we were growing up, not because we didn't crave the knowledge—but no one who was diagnosed and is thankful that the information was withheld. Most people I've known have been relieved to know that it wasn't just their fault that they couldn't just be like everyone else. To find out that there were other people with similar challenges who were okay.

3. Yes, labels can carry stigma. But it's the stigma that's wrong, not the fact that a word exists to describe some facet of how your brain works.

Not knowing the word "autistic" will not make your child not autistic, and it will not protect them from the mistreatment that frequently follows being autistic. I carried no label of a disability for most of my life, yet most of the same things happened to me as to people who did.

If what you really fear is that your child will be marginalized or mistreated for being autistic, then fight the marginalization, misinformation, bigotry, and dehumanizing stereotypes with us.

The burden of a stigmatized identity or disability label is difficult, but the burden of a void of missing knowledge about yourself, is much worse.

4. Knowing how to describe why things are harder for you is not "using it as an excuse."

Knowing why certain things are hard for you (and other things are easier) is vital to good decision-making about how to use the resources of time, energy, and cognitive bandwidth that you have. And also to constructive thinking about how to come up with workarounds and good strategies for things that you want to learn to do.

That I didn't know and couldn't tell anyone why things were so hard for me, did not make them less hard. It did not make me magically able to just do things the way everyone else did. It made me a lot more anxious, guilty, resentful, and frightened to ever put myself in a situation in which I didn't know if I'd be able to do what was expected of me.

Being able to recognize what's a productive use of your internal resources, and what isn't, is a vital skill when you're seeking to live sustainably with a disability or major cognitive difference. Neurological boundaries don't disappear because you lack the words to describe them. Disregarding or pushing past those boundaries is a useful thing to be able to do sometimes, but having to do it constantly and relentlessly is no way to build a life.

5. Having community is pretty much the best thing.

There's a lot about being autistic that most professionals, teachers, or therapists don't know anything about. Or even if they do, they can't know what the internal, subjective experience is. So practically the only way to get perspective or help from someone who knows exactly what you're talking about, is to talk to other autistic people. From certain sensory, cognitive, and emotional experiences; making self-care skills manageable; organizational strategies; making your habitat friendly and interdependent living; useful use of scripted language; overload, shutdowns; the reality of midlife breakdowns and loss of abilities later in life (because yes, this can happen at any time in our lives, not just early childhood); to differences in how we experience time, memory, sexuality and gender…to just being able to share obsessions and pleasures like cats and trains and things lined up in rows with mutual passion. It is really, really good to be able to talk to other autistic people about things.

Sometimes it's just nice to talk to someone who talks or thinks like you.

I also have autistic friends who aren't part of the online/advocacy communities, and that's fine. Some people decide they don't need or want that community in the same way, and that's their decision to make. But they can't make an informed decision if they don't have the relevant information.

6. They will figure it out anyway.

We have the internet, and because autistic people write about our lives all the time, in blogs and books and poetry and song, they will stumble across something that accurately describes what their life feels like in a way that nothing else ever has.

At somewhere between 1% and 2% of the population, we are everywhere, and they'll meet one of us, and someone will tell them the truth.

We are characters in books, movies, plays, and popular television shows. There are more and more chances that they will see themselves accurately represented, and put it together.

I had to figure it out myself (though not without help, but that's another story). It took me 28 years, and it consumed me utterly. I could never get on with living my life in certain ways until I knew. I will probably spend the rest of my life trying to describe, trying to tell the truth, about what exactly that lack of knowledge did to me. I'm 31 now and I'm not even close.

Walking down the street and feeling like the world makes sense is a feeling I'm still getting used to.

> *"Harder to express how that break becomes healed, a bone once fractured, now whole, but different from the bone never broken. And harder still to follow the path between the two."* — Eli Clare

...and when they do figure it out, and realize that you knew and withheld the information, both of you will have to deal with that breach of trust.

I'm thankful, at least, that my parents genuinely didn't know, that they were actually misinformed and clueless, that even if I still think they were somewhat in denial, they weren't lying to me. If they had been, and I had ever learned that they'd deliberately denied the information to me, I don't know that I'd ever forgive them for that.

And while I'm as proud of figuring it out for myself as I am of anything I've ever done, it's not something I would put someone through if I could help it. You can help it. There's so much more of life to live than having to wrench the most basic facts about yourself out of the fabric of the universe.

❖ ❖ ❖

Alyssa Hillary

Alyssa is an Autistic writer, scholar, and activist. Sie does work in disability studies with a focus on issues affecting sier fellow autistic people and how different views on disability affect technology use related to disability. Alyssa blogs at Yes, That Too, *self-publishes some of sier own short fiction, and has work in the books* Typed Words, Loud Voices, Criptiques, *and* The Queens Readers: A Collection of Essays on the Words and Worlds of Tamora Pierce. *When not doing any of those things, Alyssa is a graduate student in mathematics and enjoys playing Ultimate Frisbee.*

I find Alyssa's blog, *Yes, That Too*[1], a fascinating place. Alyssa is smart and thoughtful and these traits show in sier writing style and in the topics sie chooses to write about.

The issue of language is one that parents of Autistic children will all eventually come up against. There is a debate that rears its head frequently in the Autism community around how we refer to Autistic people, and whether we should use person-first language or identity-first language.

Alyssa writes on the topic of language succinctly and with clarity. I value sier opinion, because as a non Autistic parent I do not feel it is my place to decide how my children should use language to speak about their identity. I would much rather listen to Autistic people who have spoken about this and let my kids know how others who share their neurology feel about it, then leave the kids to decide.

In fact, that is exactly what we did a while back, and both the kids decided they would like to be referred to as Autistic. It was, particularly for my son, an empowering experience. I hope reading

---

1.   http://yesthattoo.blogspot.com.au

Alyssa's thoughts gives other parents the confidence to do the same.

Autism and Language

Alyssa Hillary

I have a bit of a complicated relationship with language in general, but when it comes to describing my disabilities, it's fairly straightforward. I'm Autistic. I do not have autism, nor am I a person with autism, and I probably wouldn't care nearly as much about the distinction if there weren't parents and professionals touting person-first language all over the place, insisting that autism doesn't define us and trying really hard to separate the person from the autism.

The reason I don't think I'd care that much is that I don't care that much about language when it comes to most of my other defining characteristics. (And I say other defining characteristics because I have quite a few, of which *autism is one*.) I don't care if people say I have brown hair or if they call me a brunette. I don't care if people say I have brown eyes or that I am brown-eyed. I don't care if people say that I'm someone who likes to write or that I'm a writer, though I very rarely hear anyone saying the former. It takes more words to say most things in person-first language in English.

But.

Many non-autistic people who think they know what the best and most respectful thing to call me is *do* insist on person-first language around autism. One reason I see a lot is that "we need to remember that I'm a person first." I have a complicated relationship with that idea, too. It sounds a bit like they're trying to ignore the importance of autism in my life, for one thing. For another, "autistic person" includes the word "person" just as much as "person with autism" does, so it should be just as effective at reminding people that I am, in fact, a person. Lastly and most importantly, if someone has trouble remembering that I am a person without using a language trick about it, *I don't want them anywhere near me*. I even less want them near people who are at more significant risks than I am from dehumanization!

Another thing I see is insistence that autism doesn't define me. I know they mean well here, and I think they mean that autism isn't my *only* important characteristic (or even a single characteristic,) but there's a problem here. The problem is that autism *is* a defining trait for me. It's pervasive, and it's defining, and using a false statement to argue that I should call myself a "person with autism" just isn't going to work.

Perhaps they mean that autism *shouldn't* define me, but why shouldn't it? No one takes issue when I call myself a mathematician or a writer or an engineer or an artist or a singer, all identity-first terms and mostly less defining than "autistic" is for me. ("Mathematician" is the only one that might beat "Autistic" outright, but the two are so strongly linked for me that it doesn't make much sense to compare them.) I think this comes from people viewing autism as inherently negative, from viewing disability as inherently negative, even if they don't want to admit to it. It ties in with narratives of "overcoming" disability and of doing things despite one's disabilities.

I can't identify with narratives of overcoming autism or doing things despite autism, and I won't choose my language to match the narratives someone else wants me to identify with.

The last bit is that "person with autism" sometimes sounds to me like we're calling the autism detachable from the person. That's not how it works, but we run into lots of problems when people try to *act* like it works that way. Parents trying to "recover" their children from autism, trying to separate the autism from their children, has quite a bit of history and unfortunately continues. Professionals still consider the "optimal" outcome to be us "losing our diagnoses," even if we're really trading "autism" for "anxiety and depression." Being the best people we can be, autism and all, isn't on the agenda nearly so often as trying to hide the autism we're "with" is, and that's a problem.

Autism is pervasive. There isn't some non-autistic version of me hidden under layers of autism, or even a nice way to draw a line between me and the autism. There's an Autistic me with a personality and interests and friends, all of which I relate to in an Autistic way.

❖ ❖ ❖

Cynthia Kim

Cynthia Kim is the proud owner of many labels including woman, wife, mother, writer, editor, entrepreneur and, most recently, autistic. Diagnosed with Asperger's syndrome in her early forties, she began blogging about life on the spectrum at MusingsofanAspie.com. She is the author of two books on her experiences, Nerdy, Shy and Socially Inappropriate: A User Guide to an Asperger Life *and* I Think I Might Be Autistic: A Guide to Autism Spectrum Disorder Diagnosis and Self-Discovery for Adults. *When she isn't writing, she can often be found running or hiking backwoods trails somewhere on the east coast of the US.*

Cynthia's blog, Musings of an Aspie[1], is one of the most brilliant resources for parents of Autistic children. I go there regularly to see what she has to say on a variety of topics, from language and behaviour to emotions, cognitive function, and sensory processing.

I first came across Cynthia's blog in 2013 when someone shared one of her articles about stimming with me. I was encouraged and reassured to find someone explaining in easy to understand ways why it is so important to let our kids do what they need to in order to regulate both the sensory input they experience and the emotions they feel.

I was so pleased when Cynthia agreed that I could republish her words in this book. The article is called "Socially Inappropriate," and follows this introduction. The next chapter is a reprint of Cynthia's article, "The High Cost of Self-Censoring (or Why Stimming Is a Good Thing)." I hope these two articles together here will help others as much as they have helped me.

---

1.   http://musingsofanaspie.com

Socially Inappropriate

Cynthia Kim

Socially appropriate.

This innocuous phrase has turned obnoxious for me. Here's an example of why: I'm reading a book about teaching social skills to children with Asperger's and I come across a sentence stating that children should be allowed time to engage in stress-reducing activities, including "self-stimulation in socially appropriate forms."

What sort of stimming is socially appropriate, you may wonder? The book doesn't say. Presumably everyone knows? Later in the book I find a clue. There is a list of sample relaxation activities that children can try as a way to de-escalate their stress. One of the activities is "rocking in private."

Does that mean rocking is socially inappropriate? I assume so, since it's meant to be done in secret only. How about flapping? Bouncing? Spinning? Playing with a stim toy? Rubbing a surface? Staring at a moving object?

Where does the line between socially appropriate and socially inappropriate lie? Who decides?

❖ ❖ ❖

Actually, the idea of an adult thinking a child is complying with the rule that they are only "allowed" to stim in private is kind of funny.

Is the child chewing on something, manipulating something with their hands or fingers, touching something, kicking their feet, clicking their tongue, chewing their lip, rubbing their blankie, petting their favorite stuffed toy, sniffing their food, fisting their hands in their pockets, twirling their hair, watching the ceiling fan? All forms of stimming.

Oh, you mean *stimming*.

Stimming: repetitive activity that makes an autistic person look like a freak.

When I read some of the ways non-autistic people talk about stimming, I swear this is the definition they have in their heads.

❖ ❖ ❖

Oh, wait, I know: socially inappropriate stims are ones that draw attention to us. If you rock in public, people will stare.

And whose problem is that?

Try out these sentences instead:

If you sign in public, people will stare.

If you use your wheelchair in public, people will stare.

If you limp in public, people will stare.

If you use your assistance dog in public, people will stare.

And if people do stare, other people will think they're rude. Who would tell a Deaf person not to sign in public, or a paraplegic not to use their wheelchair in public?

But people tell autistic kids not to stim in public all the time. Again and again I see conversations and articles insisting that stimming—or if they're trying to be politically correct, *certain types of stimming*—isn't appropriate public behavior.

Really? And why is that? Who exactly does stimming embarrass? Not the autistic person who's doing it.

❖ ❖ ❖

Stimming happens. It's not something autistic people choose to do.

Controlling it is like playing whack-a-mole. Stop it over here and it's just going to pop back up over there. Whack it enough times and it's going to go underground and rip up your entire yard.

❖ ❖ ❖

The High Cost of Self-Censoring (or Why Stimming is a Good Thing)

Cynthia Kim

As an autistic adult, I often feel that I need to self-censor in social situations. Don't say the wrong thing. Don't stare at people. (But don't forget to make eye contact!) Don't laugh at the wrong time. Don't speak too loudly or too softly or too often or too infrequently. And above all, don't stim.

Stimming makes people nervous. As a kid, I stimmed like mad. I've been rewatching old home movies and there I am stimming my way through Santa's Land and Disney World and every birthday party ever. I'm bouncing, rocking, twitching, flapping, hopping. I'm hammering with anything that remotely resembles a hammer and rubbing my fingers over every nearby surface. I'm constantly in motion.

Four decades later, my stimming is more discreet. You'd have to be watching closely to notice that I'm rubbing my thumbs over the spacebar on my keyboard when I stop typing. Or that I'm fidgeting with a bottle cap under the table at a restaurant or playing with my hair while driving or folding and unfolding a piece of paper while I wait in the bank.

Stimming is so much a part of who I am that I when first read about autistic traits, I completely denied that I have stims.

That little kid in the home movies grew into a teenager who learned to stim more subtly to avoid drawing attention to herself. I've found socially acceptable stims like doodling or manipulating objects (pen, stress ball, cell phone) with my hands. I've tucked away my more obvious stims for use in private.

Well, mostly. The day of my Asperger's assessment, I started out stimming discreetly during the interview with the psychologist. By the time I hit the three-hour mark in testing, I found myself rocking back and forth as I tried to work out the spatial reasoning puzzles.

There is too much comfort in stimming—it's too much of a biological imperative—for me to completely extinguish it.

I recently read that medicating a child to reduce stimming is a good way to help the child concentrate on school work. But I have a feeling that the medication does more to make the people around the child feel better. If anything, stimming improves my concentration. It's a release, like sneezing or scratching an itch. Have you ever tried to ignore an itch? What if someone told you it was wrong to scratch yourself to relieve an itch? What would that do for your concentration?

Stereotyped Movement (Stereotypies)

Stimming is the most common term used to describe the repetitive movements characteristic of autism, but a more formal term (and the one used in the DSM diagnostic criteria) is *stereotyped movement* or *stereotypies*. In this case, "stereotyped" has a different meaning than the one we're used to. In a behavioral science capacity, stereotyped movement refers to repetitive, nonfunctional movement.

Like so much of what the experts term "nonfunctional" about autistic behavior, I'd ask: nonfunctional for whom?

A Little Insight from our Primate Cousins

Trying to understand what stereotypic movement is and why it happens led me to reading about stereotypic behavior in captive animals. In an issue of *Laboratory Primate Newsletter* (Volume 23, No 4, October 2004) I found a surprising answer.

The researchers concluded that stereotypic behaviors in captive animals aren't truly abnormal; they're a reaction to *abnormal environmental conditions*. In other words, monkeys should spend their days swinging from trees and running about in the jungle, not sitting in small cages. When the monkeys can't indulge their natural behavioral tendencies, they resort to stereotypical movements like "pacing back and forth, running in circles, somersaulting, rocking, self-biting, earpulling, hair-pulling, eye-poking, etc."

Sound familiar?

The article goes on to say:

"Many stereotypies are signs of frustration, with the subject being chronically thwarted from expressing basic activities."

Yes, stereotypies are related to *frustration at being chronically thwarted from expressing basic activities.*

Think about all of the things that feel like basic needs to an autistic. Being immersed in a special interest for long periods of time. Being alone. Sticking to routines. Avoiding excessive noise, strong smells, or crowds. How often do we feel thwarted when trying to pursue the things we find comforting? *Chronically* seems like a pretty good description to me.

When you look at it from the perspective of the animal researchers, autistics are engaging in stimming (stereotypies) not because we're abnormal but because we're constantly at odds with our environment.

While it's impossible for the majority of us to indulge our autistic tendencies 24/7, it's important to recognize the cost of self-censoring. When I'm happy, the urge to bounce up and down is nearly irrepressible. I've learned that it's okay to bounce when I'm with my family. In fact, my husband's reaction to my unbridled, childlike joy is often a huge smile. It makes him happy to see me happy, even if my way of showing it is more "appropriate" to a four-year-old than a forty-three-year-old.

Self-censoring is exhausting. Letting my autistic side rule feels liberating. Why would I want to extinguish that?

Kassiane Sibley

Kassiane Sibley is a vintage 1982 Autistic, diagnosed in 1986. She has been doing Autistic activism since 1999 or so and currently blogs at Radical Neurodivergence Speaking *and* We Are Like Your Child. *Kassiane is currently attending university with every intention of dragging the neuroscience community kicking and screaming into the neurodiversity paradigm. She has two seizure-detecting cats named after things found in the brain.*

I like people who say it like it is. So, I like Kassiane.

She is a fierce advocate and activist whose writing cuts right to the heart of the matter.

I also like that she makes no apology for the fact that what she has to say makes people uncomfortable. Indeed, I believe that people *should* be uncomfortable about the things Kassiane says because she consistently—and rightly—challenges negative attitudes toward Autistic people and the way they exist.

Kassiane's writing often moves me to tears—sometimes of frustration, sometimes anger, sometimes sadness. She always challenges me to think about things from a viewpoint I haven't seen before. You can find Kassiane's blog at timetolisten.blogspot.com.

In this article she writes candidly, as a survivor of ABA "therapy," about what it has cost her to be forced as a child to appear "indistinguishable" from her peers.

The Cost of Indistinguishability is Unreasonable

Kassiane Sibley

With apologies/thanks to Beth of Love Explosions *for the perfect title.*

The cost of indistinguishability is unreasonable, as my past few weeks have kind of proven.

I don't even know where to start so I will start, I guess, at the beginning.

Once upon a time a small dark-haired, dark-eyed baby girl was born to a mom and a last name donor and a dad who wouldn't find out about her for a few years. As this baby grew into a little girl, her mom noticed she grew up differently from the other little girls and boys. She didn't talk. She couldn't be separated from books. She didn't look people in the face. She didn't respond as expected to things being said to her.

So this little girl was taken by her mother and last name donor to a doctor who diagnosed autism and proposed the parents sign her up for an exciting new therapy, one that might make children indistinguishable from peers. And they did.

And although the child shoved an M&M up a therapist's nose when they told her to touch nose (whose nose??), by kindergarten she was speaking, was plainly academically capable, had a rather large vocabulary from reading, and was "table ready." So they sent this little girl to kindergarten with no supports.

But this little girl was still Autistic. She was just academically indistinguishable from peers, or at least distinguishable in a socially acceptable way. So this little girl did not get nearly the help she needed.

Instead this little girl was told that every problem ever was her own choice because she chose to be strange. This little girl was told that everyone needs and wants friends, but was not told how "friends" works.

She was taught that friends works by when people want you to do things, she had do them for them. And then they will be your friend.

But she doesn't get to ask things of them, they are tolerating her and that is their end of the deal. She is weird and loathsome and deserves every bad thing that ever could possibly happen to her because she cannot choose to be normal.

So she kind of almost made friends, ish, by doing things for people. Whatever they asked. At least they were telling her what they wanted. If people will ask, she can make them happy.

At least she can make them happy. In theory, at least. They tell her what they want, she does it, no one is angry.

That is easy compared to home. At home she has to guess to make people happy. They won't just tell her what she needs to do to be acceptable. If she doesn't do what they wanted, they hit her or yell at her or throw her into a wall or sexually assault her to make her "respectful." If she guesses right they shower love and affection and praise. If they didn't want anything, and she manages to not do something they actively didn't want, they leave her alone.

It goes way back to "LOOK AT ME": the way to make people not hurt her is to do what they want. The way to be safe is to do what they want. People show love or friendship by not hurting her. There is nothing more. Just the all-encompassing "do what they want and I will be safe."

And as most small children do, this little girl grew up. She is 30 now. By all superficial accounts she won: she no longer has anything to do with her unpredictable parents. She lives alone. She works. She's going through college a second time in hopes of getting a degree that will allow her a dream job. She socializes. She has talents. She does activism—and is actually kind of known for it.

People know her name. This is the ultimate winning in our society. What didn't kill her made her strong, right?

Being strong means you can't be vulnerable. Being strong means you have no limits. Being strong means you can weather your own shit-shower—and oh has there ever been one—and solve everyone else's things too. Save the world and everyone in it.

But she is metaphorically drowning. Her internal model of friends is "I do what they tell me to do." No one has to be nice to her, or put up with her, so she has to do what they ask. "No" isn't an option. And the few times she has tried, "no" has been interpreted as "keep begging and I will do it."

People ask, and she does. And when people don't ask? She doesn't know what to do. The guessing is impossible. Not knowing what they want is oh so anxiety-provoking that she cannot breathe for hyperventilation. They can tell her they don't want anything, but that's never true. People always want something and the guessing game is not a thing she can do anymore.

People say they don't want anything. They always want something. Stand up, sit down, touch nose, good girl. Do my homework for me. Social media crisis this. Can you cover another shift at work? These, she understands. "Just be my friend" doesn't mean anything. She cannot deal with "just be my friend." Tell her what you want from her!

She can deal with people telling her what they want. But she can't, realistically, sustain it.

She is burned out and has nowhere to turn. Never anywhere to turn. She is who people call when the backup failed. She is strong. She isn't allowed to be burned out. That is a luxury for people who weren't tested by fire. And that is a luxury for people who can believe people don't always want something.

Her brain is telling her that people only tolerate her because she does things for them and the minute they realize she isn't the symbol of strength and endurance they built her into, they will react with hatred and violence. That is what they always do. She is not allowed a moment of weakness. The community needs her. They need her strength. They need her to be a symbol. Can't she do just this one more thing?

She never wants to hear again that she is strong. She doesn't know a way out.

Well, she knows one way out.

Because people can't demand things from you if you're dead. Not really. And when they react with hatred, what are they going to do to you? You're *dead.* They can't do anything to you.

And then there is no more guessing, there is no more guessing wrong, there are no more demands. There's no more "the common denominator in these problems is you" or "if you weren't so political you wouldn't care, the problem is that you want your rights" or "just this one thing." There's no more being shat upon because it's okay because she's "strong" and "used to it" and all the other justifications.

And she already won, right?

She's just too tired. She can't anymore. But she has to. Her worth, her right to exist, are pinned on what she does for other people to make up for being so detestably weird.

She can't do it anymore. So she is worthless. She can't she can't she can't.

This is the cost of indistinguishability. And she knows it's unreasonable intellectually, but she can't make herself believe it.

There's

always

one

more

condition

on

being

tolerated

and

this

is

unreasonable

too.

❖ ❖ ❖

Sparrow Rose Jones

Sparrow Rose Jones is a middle-aged nomadic Autistic living a life of endless discovery throughout the United States with her best friend, Fermat the Wonder Cat. She is an author, artist and composer (with books, music, and t-shirts available through her portfolio site at sparrowrose.com), as well as an amateur astronomer, naturalist, and mathematician. Her creative mission is two-fold: to celebrate the infinite diversity of life, and to help others avoid repeating her mistakes so they can go forward to make fresh and original mistakes of their own instead.

I've known Sparrow a few years now. One of the things I love most about her is the patient and gentle way she explains things. Sparrow shares her wisdom with respect and compassion. She has been a major influence in my life and has helped me become a better parent to my Autistic children.

When Sparrow agreed to allow me to republish something from her blog, *Unstrange Mind*[1], I had a dilemma on my hands. How to choose just one of her blog posts, from so many I have read and found so incredibly helpful?

In the end, I chose to include this one about ABA therapy for Autistic children, quite simply because I believe it is the best, most comprehensive piece on the subject available online. Unfortunately, therapies for Autistic children can be a contentious and controversial topic in the community of parents of Autistic children. Sparrow writes with diplomacy and from a place of genuine concern for the wellbeing of the children in her tribe.

If you would like to read more from Sparrow you can purchase her book, *No You Don't: Essays from an Unstrange Mind*, through Amazon

---

1.   URL: http://unstrangemind.wordpress.com

or through her portfolio site at sparrowrose.com.

ABA – Applied Behavior Analysis

Sparrow Rose Jones

This week, I watched an online community implode. I'm not going to talk about that, though, because it was very painful to watch people I love being treated so badly. But a lot of the implosion centered around a topic I do want to talk about. That topic is ABA—Applied Behavior Analysis, a common type of therapy for Autistic children. I watched people fight around in circles, chasing their metaphorical tails. It will take some time and lots of words to unpack this topic, but I hope you will stick with me on this because it's so important and there is a lot that needs to be understood here.

Here's the argument in a nutshell. It gets longer, angrier, and much more detailed than this, but I am exhausted just from reading the fighting, so I'm boiling it all down to two statements. And both statements are correct.

Autistic adult: "ABA is abuse."

Parent of Autistic child: "I'm not abusive and my child is benefitting greatly from ABA therapy."

You read me right: both statements are correct. That is part of what I need to unpack today. I think the best place to start is with the fact that both people above are using the term "ABA," but what they are actually talking about are usually two different things. First we need to define ABA.

Well, actually, first I want to put people at ease.

Parents—it's got to be painful to feel like a whole group of people are ganging up on you and telling you that you are abusing your child. You love your child. You want the best for your child. You are spending thousands of dollars out of pocket to try to give your child the best possible chance in life. You worry about your child. You feel like you never even knew what love was until your child came along. And if something you are doing is harming your child, you want to know about it and stop it. It hurts to be told that you are abusive toward the child you love so much.

And my fellow Autistics—you grew up feeling picked apart. You were subjected to things that harmed you. You still have PTSD today from things that may have been done with your best interests at heart but were actually quite damaging. You didn't fit in to the world around you and the adults who were charged with your care when you were growing up were stumbling around in the dark when it came to trying to figure out how to raise a child like you were. It is triggering to see that so many of the things that hurt you when you were growing up are still being said and done to and about children who are so very much like you were when you were their age. You want to stop the cycle of pain and you want children to grow up happy, healthy, and loved. It frightens and angers you to see many of the "best practices" that Autistic children today live with.

And there is a good chance that the two of you—the Autistic adult and the parent of an Autistic child—are not even talking about the same thing when you say "ABA." Major organizations (particularly Autism Speaks) have lobbied hard for Medicaid and insurance companies to cover ABA for Autistic children. As a result, many therapists now call what they do "ABA," even in cases where the actual therapy is very different from genuine ABA, in order to have their services covered by insurance. It's similar to the philosophy of therapists I've known who don't believe in diagnosing "mental illness" but put a name on their patients' struggles anyway because many insurance policies only pay for therapy if the treatment is for a diagnosis listed in the DSM. That's the main point that I wanted to make, but there's still a lot to say on this topic.

If almost everything is being called "ABA" then what is actual ABA? And why do Autistic adults say it is abusive? What sort of warning signs should parents be watching for? What is harmful about certain practices? Those are a lot of questions to answer, but I will do my best. Bear in mind that I'm not a therapist—ABA or otherwise—and I'm not a parent. I'm one Autistic adult, one person coping with therapy-induced PTSD, one person exhausted by the all-out war I see every day between people like me and people who love people like me, one person who wants to see a better world for everyone (but, I admit, especially for Autistic people.)

ABA was developed by Dr. Ivar Lovaas. As a 1965 *Life Magazine* article[1] explains, the core theory of ABA was that a therapist, "forcing a

---

1.   Grant, A. [Photographer] (1965). "Screams, Slaps & Love." *Life Magazine*. URL:
      http://neurodiversity.com/library_screams_1965.html

change in a child's outward behavior" would, "effect an inward psychological change." The article says, "Lovaas feels that by 1) holding any mentally crippled child accountable for his behavior and 2) forcing him to act normal, he can push the child toward normality."

Much has changed, but this core premise of Lovaas' work remains consistent. ABA's core belief is that forty hours per week of "therapy" geared toward making a child externally appear as "normal" as possible will "fix the brokenness" inside that made the child behave that way. ABA believes in an extreme form of "fake it until you make it," and because it is behaviorism at its most pure—that is, a psychological science that treats internal processes as irrelevant to function (Lovaas said, "you have to put out the fire first before you worry how it started")—it treats behavior as meaningless and unwanted actions rather than as communication.

This approach is troubling for many reasons.

ABA strongly emphasizes the importance of intensive, saturated therapy and insists that it is crucial to get 40 hours a week of therapy for very young children. Think for a moment how exhausted you, a grown adult, are after 40 hours of work in a week and you will begin to understand why we get so concerned about putting a three-year-old child through such a grueling schedule. Being Autistic doesn't give a three-year-old child superpowers of endurance. Forty hours a week of ABA is not just expensive, it is painfully exhausting. ABA maintains a schedule like this with the intention of breaking down a child's resistance and will.

I understand that you are afraid for your child. Their future is unknown. You are worried about their ability to live a fulfilled life. You are worried about their ability to have self-supporting work and be taken care of after you pass on. And I understand that this fear, coupled with a deep desire to give your child the best you can give them, can lead you to accept the ABA attitude of "more is better." But stop a moment and think about the capacity for sustained focus of the average three-year-old and consider what a "therapy" that tries to double (or more) that capacity is doing to a child. If you stress a child out or even traumatize them with extreme "therapies," you are paradoxically increasing the chances of incapacitating PTSD in the child's future. Yes, you want your child to develop as much as they are able to develop and you want them to enjoy their life and hopefully provide for themselves, but exhaustion and trauma are not going to aid those sorts of development.

Worse than the exhaustion of so many hours of therapy, though, is the heavy focus on making a child "indistinguishable from his peers." The main goal of ABA is to make a child *LOOK* normal. This is insidious for a few reasons. first, it is the best way to get the parents to continue to co-operate with the therapists for many years. Of course you are going to be moved to tears if the therapist gets your child to look you in the eye or say "Mommy" to you, or sit at the table and eat a meal without fidgeting or melting down. Of course you will feel like the therapist is making "progress" and "healing" your child. That is a very natural response. So you will see the progress and you will want to continue with ABA therapy and you will be very defensive when adults Autistics online suggest that what is happening in your home might be a bad thing. What was bad were struggles every mealtime. What was bad was never hearing your child's voice. What was bad were the judgmental or pitying stares you and your child got when you went out in public and people saw your child spinning around or flapping her hands or becoming so anxious you were forced to leave your groceries unpurchased and flee the store.

But if your child is getting classic ABA "therapy," what you are seeing is an illusion. What looks like "progress" is happening at the expense of the child's sense of self, comfort, feelings of safety, ability to love who they are, stress levels, and more. The outward appearance is of improvement, but with ABA, that outward improvement is married to a dramatic increase in internal anxiety and suffering.

ABA therapists are trained to find out what your child loves the most and hold it for ransom. Often, it's food. If your therapist suggests withholding food as a form of behavioral therapy, run screaming. That is harmful. If your child's therapist will not allow you to remain in the room during a session (they will usually tell you that your presence will be a distraction that will keep your child focused on you instead of on the therapy they need to be paying attention to) that is a big warning sign. If you are able to witness your child's therapy sessions and your child is spending a lot of time crying or going limp or flopping on the floor or showing signs you recognize as indicators of anxiety or fear, beware the therapy. If the therapist insists on pushing forward with the therapy when your child is crying or going limp instead of giving your child recovery time, run screaming. "Therapy" that trades your child's sense of safety in the present for a promise of future "progress" is exactly the sort of thing that Autistic adults mean when they talk about abusive therapy.

Therapy should make your child better—not traumatize them, possibly for many years, potentially for the rest of their life. A therapist might tell you that "a little crying" is a normal thing, but I was once an Autistic child and I can tell you that being pushed repeatedly to the point of tears with zero sense of personal power and knowing that the only way to get the repeated torment to end was to comply with everything that was asked of me, no matter how painful, no matter how uneasy it made me feel, no matter how unreasonable the request seemed, knowing that I had no way out of a repeat of the torment again and again for what felt like it would be the rest of my life was traumatizing to such a degree that I still carry emotional scars decades later. It doesn't matter whether the perpetrator is a therapist, a teacher, a parent, or an age-peer: bullying is bullying.

In my opinion, the goal of therapy should be to help the child live a better, happier, more functional life. Taking away things like hand flapping or spinning is not done to help the child. It is done because the people around the child are uncomfortable with or embarrassed by those behaviors. But those are coping behaviors for the child. It is very important to question why a child engages in the behaviors they do. It is very wrong to seek to train away those behaviors without understanding that they are the child's means of self-regulation.

When considering whether you have made a wise choice in what therapy you are providing your child or not, you want to always remember a few cardinal rules: behavior is communication and/or a means of self-regulation. Communication is more important than speech. Human connection is more important than forced eye contact. Trust is easy to shatter and painfully difficult to re-build. It is more important for a child to be comfortable and functional than to "look normal."

Work on things like anxiety and sensory issues first. Work on getting better sleep (both you and your child). Things like eye contact can come later, much later, and only if your child is comfortable with them. There are work-arounds. Lots of people fake eye contact. Lots of people have good lives with minimal or no eye contact. Forcing a child to do something that is deeply painful and distressing for no reason other than to make them look more normal is not just unnecessary, it is cruel.

I live two blocks from a behavioral clinic and I frequently walk several blocks out of my way to avoid walking past it because of the kinds of things I have seen when walking past the clinic. Let me tell you about the last thing I saw there, the thing that made me decide that I would rather walk an extra half-mile than risk seeing more ABA "therapy" on the sidewalk in front of the clinic.

A mother and father came out of the clinic with a little girl, around 7 years old by my best guess. Mother said, "Janie (not the actual name), look at me." Janie didn't look at her mother. The mother said to the father, "you know what to do," and the father took hold of Janie and turned her head toward mother, saying, "look at your mother, Janie." Janie resisted, turning her head away and trying to pull out of her father's hands. Mother crouched down and Father lifted Janie's whole body up, laying her across Mother's knee, face up. "Look at your mother, Janie," father said. "Look at me, Janie," Mother said. Janie began to whimper. Her body was as stiff as a board. Father held her body firm and Mother took hold of Janie's head, "look at me, Janie," Mother said.

I was glued to the sidewalk. I didn't want to see any more but I couldn't look away, couldn't walk away. Janie began to moan and thrash her body. Father's hands held her body steady as she kicked and flailed. Mother's hands held Janie's head steady. Both kept urging Janie to look at her mother. Janie's moans turned to screams but neither parent let her go.

Finally, Janie's entire body went limp with defeat. She apparently made eye contact because Mother and Father began to lavish praise on her. "Good girl, Janie. Good eye contact. Good girl. Let's get some ice cream now." Janie's limp body slid to the sidewalk where she lay, sobbing. Father picked her up and carried her to the car, the whole way praising her submission. "Good eye contact, Janie."

What did Janie learn that day? I'll give you a hint: it was not that people are more trusting of those who make good eye contact. It was not that she will appear more normal and thus fit into society better if she makes good eye contact. It wasn't even that Mom really loves it when Janie connects with her through the eyes like that.

Janie learned that adults can have whatever they want from her, even if it hurts and even if they have to hurt her to get it. Janie learned that her body does not belong to her and that she has to give others access to it at any time, for any reason, even if she wasn't doing anything that could hurt herself or others. Janie learned that there is no point in resisting and that it is her job to let others do what they want with her body, no matter how uncomfortable it makes her.

You may think I'm exaggerating or making this out to be more extreme than it is, but stop for a moment and imagine years of this "therapy." Forty hours a week of being told to touch her nose and make eye contact and have "quiet hands" and sit still. A hundred and sixty hours a month of being restrained and punished when she doesn't want to touch her nose and being given candy and praise when she does touch her nose for the 90,000th time. Nearly two thousand hours a year of being explicitly taught that she does not own her body and she does not have the right to move it in ways that feel comfortable and safe to her. How many years will she be in therapy? How many years will she be taught to be a good girl? To touch her nose on command? To make eye contact on demand? Graduating to hugs, she will be taught that she is required to hug any adult who wants a hug from her. She will be punished when she does not hug, and praised and fed when she does.

And who will protect her from the predator who wants to hug her? Who will teach her that she is only required to yield her bodily autonomy for her parents and therapists but not for strangers? What if the predator turns out to be one of her therapists or parents? How will she resist abuse when she has had so many hours of training in submission? Therapy is an investment in the future, but ABA therapy is creating a future for Janie of being the world's doormat. Is that the future Janie's parents want for her?

If your child's therapist believes it is more important for your child to comply with every command than to have any control at all over his or her body, run screaming. And don't forget that a layer of training does not change the underlying neurology. ABA uses the same methods and theories as dog training and if I train my dog to shake hands, it doesn't make him more human. It just makes him a dog who can shake hands. Similarly, if you train an Autistic to make eye contact and not flap their hands and say "I love you, too" and stay on task, it just makes them into an Autistic who can fake being not-autistic with some relative measure of success. Underneath the performance is still an Autistic brain and an Autistic nervous system and it is very important to remember that. Being trained to hide any reaction to painful noises, smells, lights, and feelings doesn't make the pain go away. Imagine years of living with pain that you have been trained to hide. How long would it last before you broke down? Some Autistics last an amazingly long time before they break down and burn out.

And intensive ABA therapy will also teach a child that there is something fundamentally wrong and unacceptable about who they are. Not only is that child trained to look normal, they are trained to hate who they are inside. They are trained to hate who they are and hide who they are. They will work very hard to hide who they are, because they have learned to hate who they are. And as a result, they will push themselves to the brink of destruction. And when they finally crumble from years of hiding their sensory pain and years of performing their social scripts and blaming themselves every time a script doesn't carry them successfully through a social situation, they will be angry at themselves and blame themselves for their nervous breakdown.

All those years of ABA therapy will have taught them that they are fundamentally wrong and broken; that they are required to do everything authority demands of them (whether it's right or wrong for them); that they are always the one at fault when anything social goes wrong; that they get love, praise, and their basic survival needs met so long as they can hide any trace of autism from others; that what they want doesn't matter.

Now you know what to watch for. Your child's therapist may use the term "ABA" in order to get paid, but they might not be doing these harmful, degrading, abusive things to your child at all. If your child's therapist is respecting your child, not trying to break down the child's sense of self and body-ownership, treating behavior as communication rather than pointless motions that need to be trained away, valuing speech but not at the expense of communication, giving your child breaks to recover and not over-taxing their limited focusing abilities . . . then they can call their therapy anything they want to, but it is not ABA. (And hold on to that therapist! They are golden!)

And I hope that the next time you hear an Autistic adult say that ABA is abuse, you are compassionate. Remember the suffering so many of us endured. Know that we say those things because we love your children and want to help them. We do not say them because we hate you and want to call you abusers. We don't hate you at all and we want to help you. Sometimes we are clumsy in how we go about it, because, well, we are Autistic and communication difficulties are part of that package. But know that when we attack ABA, we are not intending to attack you. We want your child to sleep through the night and laugh with joy and become toilet-trained (on whatever schedule their bodies can handle—don't forget that we tend to be late bloomers), and have a healthy, happy, productive, love-filled life.

We want you to rejoice in parenting and connect with your children on a deep and meaningful level. When an Autistic adult says "ABA is abuse," you might be tempted to hear, "you are abusing your child." But that is not what we are saying. Next time you hear an Autistic adult say "ABA is abuse," please hear those words as, "I love you and your child. Be careful! There are unscrupulous people out there who will try to convert the fear you feel for your child's future into money in their pocket, at the cost of your child's well-being."

And if you are a therapist and you are upset when we say "ABA is abuse," know that we are not talking about you . . . unless you are using shock punishments or making children endure long hours of arduous therapy beyond their ability to cope or teaching children that they do not have the right to say who can have access to intimacy with their body or not (and forced eye contact is a particularly nasty violation of a person's control over their bodily intimacy). If you are not the kind of therapist who we are talking about when we talk about the harm of therapy, then we are not talking about you! Thank you for being one of the good guys. We need more like you. Teach others what you know. Spread the love and help change the world, please!

Thank you for reading all of this. I know it was a lot of words, but this is such an important topic. Children are the future and I don't have words to explain how painful it is when I see Autistic adults being verbally bullied and abused because they are trying to help the children by helping parents to understand more about the lived experience of autism and more about the kinds of things that can be very harmful to Autistic lives.

I had over a decade of therapy in my childhood and much of it was not good therapy and I am significantly damaged because of it. When I say ABA is abuse—when we Autistic adults say ABA is abuse—we are speaking from a collective wisdom gained through painful experiences that have left lasting scars on us. We don't want anyone else to have to go through the pain we have gone through. Please respect where we are coming from and please do not add to the trauma by attacking us for trying to help others. Thank you.

Michael Scott Monje, Jr.

Michael Scott Monje, Jr. is a West Michigan writer whose work centers on neurodivergent and LGBT characters. They write the Shaping Clay *blog, which publishes a web serial featuring an autistic child growing up in the late 1980s and early 1990s. They are also the author of three novels:* Nothing is Right, Mirror Project, *and* Defiant, *as well as the ebook* A Waking Narrative.

Reading Michael's words, although they do not particularly pertain to issues of parenting my young children, has given me the gift of insight into the sorts of challenges my children might face as adults. The knowledge of the struggles Autistic adults face in their lives gives parents of young children a chance to look forward, and even to plan ahead somewhat.

The other gift Michael's writing gives me is that it makes way for a dialogue that is very different from the mainstream discourse around Autism. Michael speaks plainly about the challenges they face, at the same time speaking openly and without pretence about the solutions they have found for those challenges.

For all these reasons, and more, I am really pleased to be able to share Michael's essay "Not that Autistic" with you. It was originally published on Michael's website, but has been updated for this book. You can find Michael's site, *Shaping Clay*, at mmonjejr.com. To buy their books, visit the Autonomous Press website at autpress.com.

Not That Autistic

Michael Scott Monje, Jr.

Sometimes, well-meaning but clueless people tell me that I must either be "not that autistic" or "mild," or some such diminishing qualifier and not simply "autistic." They do it because they don't instantly clue in to my condition pre-disclosure. It happened a lot more when my diagnosis was fairly new, when I was first disclosing to my peers and coworkers, than it does now. In a couple of cases, I even had family members that tried to tell me that my diagnosis was mistaken or that they did not see the traits, and since they'd known me so long, they would have picked up on them.

This essay is not about them. I don't harbor any long-term ill feelings about people who had one image of me finding it difficult to adjust their image. I understand that some level of cognitive dissonance is bound to happen during this transitional time, as they revise their appraisals of some of my eccentric behaviors and they come to see things that they thought were preferences or choices as compulsions and/or automatic behaviors. That's fine. I don't even harbor ill will toward the family members who tried to convince me that my diagnosis was wrong. After all, the fact that they failed to notice that I needed help for so long probably made my disclosure seem a little like an accusation. If so, they were wrong to interpret it that way, but I understand how they did. I still think their impulses were irrational, and even if I don't point it out in the moment, I resist their judgments because these are the same people who characterized my meltdowns and inability to talk as "tantrums" and who threatened to treat me like a baby if I wanted to act like one. They are not the ones that had to cover the holes my head left in the wall with posters. And notably, though I am not close with my father, he has never questioned my diagnosis to my face. Having to repair those holes probably convinced him of my identity long before I had a word for it.

This essay is not about those moments, though. It is about the people who tell me that I must not be "that autistic" because I speak in public for a living, dress professionally, and manage to make it through the work day without flapping my hands and fidgeting... that they can see. It's about the people who think that my ability to clamp down on every impulse, conscious and subconscious, that my body is screaming at me to indulge in, is somehow the same as not feeling those impulses. People who think that my ability to *ignore* my tendencies as a way of managing them is the same as my *not experiencing those aspects of existence.*

I'm well aware that my willpower and my training, some of which was quite painful to me, sets me apart from some Autistics. I'm not trying to say that I have exactly the same challenges that someone who needs AAC or facilitated communication full-time has. I know that the fact that I can detect the flight of my language, that I can power through broken English even when my head feels like it's been run over by a steamroller, and that my most visible impairment still looks like dithering with my smartphone, that all of those things convey a privilege. I also know that there is such a thing as being visibly autistic —having muscle weakness that leads to posture, gross motor control, and other issues that make your condition unmistakable under all circumstances. And I am aware that it is a *privilege* that I am able to artificially hold my face, for hours at a time, in a pose that hides the drooping sack of flesh over my right eye, the fact that my eyes are not symmetrical or even, and the sideways twist my mouth likes to make on just one side that leaves the other one partially open. At home, and in quiet moments, I relax into it, but I know that many, many others do not have the muscle strength to hold their facial expressions in postures that not only communicate emotional meaning, but hide lopsided muscle weakness.

That does not make the issues I have to deal with less important, though. Especially not to me. It does not help improve things for people who need alternative communications technologies, facilitated communication, and other accommodations when people assume that my case is qualitatively "better" than theirs. It robs them of agency. It turns the "visibly autistic" into victims, categorizing them in such a way that it reduces expectations for their outcomes and for the goals that their educators, parents, and physical therapists will set. Not all of us can be Temple Grandin or John Elder Robison, but most of us will never know how close we can get if we are marginalized.

Oddly, it is my communication with people who are usually perceived as "more autistic" than me that is usually easiest for me to accomplish. This is because, between us, I often feel like I can acknowledge my privilege as an autistic that is capable of "passing" for short periods of time, whereas when I am around a mostly non-autistic peer group, I often feel as if I have to defend my diagnosis to keep them from running roughshod (inadvertently or not) over my needs. When I am around others like myself, no matter which symptoms they experience or the severity of those symptoms in comparison to myself, I feel like we can understand each other, and I feel less self-conscious about what I am able to do (and what I am not).

Part of my goal in all of my writing is to shed some light on the long-term difficulties inherent in being mostly invisible. This is not to claim that my challenges are "more" than those of other autistics. Instead, it is to add my voice to a choir. A choir that, as of now, is not fully representative of the range our voices should have.

We need to take a page from intersectional feminism, as a community. We need to acknowledge that symptoms, living conditions, and outside demographics such as race/ethnicity, socioeconomic status, and gender have a significant effect on our experiences as autistics. This is something that the transgender community has been much more successful than the Autistic community at articulating. It is something that the Autistic community should learn how to do, because it is useful. It shows that understanding can not come through an approved narrative, because that narrative is not truly representative of the range of problems we face and the ways that our privileges (and lack of them) can complicate our challenges.

We need more blogs, more participation, and more space given to the "visibly autistic," especially those who are nonspeakers, whose use of alternative communication like typing, letter boards, and other technological aids forces a recognition of their distinction, and the unique benefits and challenges posed by it. We need discussion that centers around our unique range of sexualities and perceptions of gender (something that, luckily, the Neuroqueer movement has started to give us).

We need to stop letting the conversation be dictated by the parents who are focused on the challenges that parenting and caregiving (sometimes for the entire lives of their children) are posing to their lifestyles and long-term goals. Their experiences are important, and their voices need to be included, but their agendas are not our own. Neither are the agendas of the "shiny" or "pretty" autistics who mostly fit in. Their stories are mostly being shared already. It will hurt us in the long run if we allow the public perception of autism to be divided between the "low functioning" and the "high functioning" simply because some people who do not consider themselves disabled by being autistic wish to have a special term for themselves that divides them from those who do. There is a vast, expansive terrain in between those viewpoints that needs to be charted, one that I am confident will reveal itself to be more about parenting, access to resources, income, racial inequity, bullying and the protection from it, and opportunities to grow naturally into ourselves, than about intrinsic "functioning" or some other ineffable quality of the brain that creates a magic divide.

In fact, being poor, but white, read as male for most of my life, and educated, I can distinctly point out the ways that academic deadline flexibility, personal favors, and social networks both provided me opportunities and denied me access to them. I am most likely a homeowner today because of a combination of family wealth and access to an income that did not require regular hours-keeping, and that employment was found through my access to higher education. At the same time, not understanding the ways that I would need to build and maintain contacts, or the political realities of attempting to move into full-time work in higher education, has left me in a position where I teach roughly one and a half times a full course load while publishing in multiple outlets per year, turning out thousands of words of freelance marketing copy per week, and running several websites for clients, for a grand total of about half of the minimum salary of a full-time assistant professor at my alma mater.

Being Autistic got me into a low-paying academic job, because it gave me the extra edge when it came to commitment, perseverance, and memory retention, but it also became the reason I never left the low-paying part behind, since my ignorance of my situation led to my not knowing that I should pursue certain resources or work to improve skills in areas where I lacked them. It did not need to be this way, though. Most of my impairments come from a combination of immersive memories of past traumas and a lack of proper occupational education and practice. Earlier knowledge about myself, coupled with a more fitting school environment and parents whose approach to discipline was not rooted in a core belief in humiliation and shame as pedagogical tools, would have allowed me to flex into a position more fitting to my skills, as many other Autistic professionals with my level of sensory impairments have already done.

I am occupying this uneasy terrain between the visible Autistic I could be if I had the ability to relax my body, and the professional who blends into the background because my environment so suits my needs that my impairments are less perceptible. This terrain needs to be charted by those of us who keep eyes on the way that our other life circumstances affect our ability to access support, resources, and even diagnosis. We need to be ready to discuss challenges without playing the "more disabled than thou" game. We need to value each others' voices, and we need to be open to discussing the private aspects of our experience that do not have a place in the current narrative. Some of us are parents. Some of us are even parents of autistic children, and we are facing a peculiar crossroads wherein we must balance our own disabilities against the needs of our children, and we must make choices about how to guide their perceptions of themselves as they construct their identities. You do not need to have a story like mine to belong in this space—it is wide and open, and its boundaries on either side are flexible and dictated more by the outsiders who visit than by the people who live here.

Let me kick things off by re-introducing myself. The last time I wrote an introductory post, I didn't quite have the distance from my diagnosis or the vocabulary to do this right:

My name is Michael, and I'm autistic. I'm not comfortable saying "I have Asperger's" or calling myself "high-functioning." I have had ritualized behaviors that cause me to lose days and sometimes weeks to compulsive video game playing, sorting and re-sorting collections like my books and vinyl records, and even occasionally exercising to exhaustion. Today, I am capable of putting that repetition to use by making web pages and performing the detail-oriented tasks of publication like typesetting the book you are currently holding—but breaking my natural perceptive qualities and need for both physical and mental stimulation to those tasks was a personal endeavor that took years and regular chemical intervention, neither of which worked until I was determining the course of them for myself.

I can talk for extended periods, but the more tired I get, the more my speech impediment slips out. It starts as a stutter, then I go tonally flat, and eventually I lose control over my enunciation and start to sound like the stereotypical autistic that most people think about because of television and the popular imagination. Usually I also get frustrated and have a hard time keeping myself from shouting when this happens, because I stop being able to say the words I intend to say, and instead I insert similar-sounding but incorrect words, like saying "speak" when I mean "steep." When it gets really bad, I will be able to see the word in my mind's eye, as if I was silently reading, but I will not know how to say it out loud. After that, I will spray syllables that usually sound like intelligent speech to others, but that I am often unaware of the content of in the moment, as my attention is not on the things my mouth is doing but on the importance of keeping my limbs under control, so that I do not flail, hit myself, or fall to the floor. I know that if I fail in that endeavor, that it is very likely I will be considered irrational. Being six feet four inches tall, as well as two hundred and ninety pounds, it is also true that many people would regard me as dangerous if that control broke. As a result, I have often said or agreed to things that are expressly against my wishes in an attempt to flee a situation, and often I have not been aware of it until the consequences of those actions return to me.

When I was younger, I had a severe problem with self-injuring. This included cutting myself with a razor, a sharpened pencil, a pen knife, or even a sharpened mattress coil. Many people thought that I was a teenager acting out by cutting myself when I did this. Those same people failed to notice that when I was a small child I would beat my head against the wall, punch myself in the head and chest, and dig at my skin with my fingernails. As a teenager, I picked up the habit of cutting because it allowed me to self-harm while blending into the expectations my peers and parents had. Ironically, my cutting was usually written off as attention-seeking when it was actually attention-avoiding. I have successfully avoided cutting since I was 21 years old, and I have avoided other forms of self-injury for seven years now (with the exception of the occasional wall punch). It took breaking the fine bones in my right hand on a concrete floor to finally give me the willpower to resist those compulsions.

I have no trouble finding work or meeting my employers'

expectations for performance, I have never been fired for failing to report on time or for breaking the rules, and my employee evaluations are never less than average. I've also never been offered a full-time benefits-eligible position, and no one can rightly explain why. I have even had people express their exasperation at my inability to obtain one while occupying positions that would allow them to offer me employment (and not doing so). I've had other people, including some I still work for, honestly do their best to coach me and to help me into the job market, but still fail to get me over that final hurdle.

I published my own book because it was easier to learn to do my own copy editing, layout, marketing, and to manage my own distribution channels than it was for me to navigate the social waters of seeking an agent and submitting work. I'm also working on starting my own retail business because teaching myself accounting, marketing, and the basic mathematics necessary to estimate my reselling markup on antiques and collectibles was easier than continuing to apply for jobs.

If people talk to me for longer than thirty minutes, even if they switch off and it's not all one conversation, I will start to noticeably twitch and to look for an escape. If you want me to prepare your quarterly tax return, I will do the entire thing without needing a break and then ask what else I can help you with.

I work a series of part-time and freelance jobs right now because they allow me to avoid being out of the house for more than four hours, because it makes me intensely uncomfortable and tired to be in the workplace for a full day. I can work six twelve hour days per week without losing focus on my writing so long as I get to make my own hours, nap when I feel overwhelmed, and avoid having to speak out loud.

Oh, yeah... that talking thing. I do it flawlessly for short periods and passably for longer ones, but I don't like it. If I was allowed, I would teach by projecting a blank Word document, and I would take questions from students and type the answers. I find it less awkward to do that, and I can type faster than I talk. I don't try to do that, though, because my career as a teacher is not about my making the classroom more comfortable and accessible for me, it's about my making my classroom more accessible and more comfortable for my students.

Until my late twenties I did not know why the world was so difficult for me to navigate, or why people who admitted to being less talented than I when they wanted to flatter me seemed to have no trouble gaining access to resources that seemed to be behind insurmountable barriers to me. Partially this was because I was not recognizably out of my depth in terms of life skills until my teen years, and by then my father was divorcing my bipolar mother while his business failed out from under him. I spent several years taking care of my siblings, and then I left home at the age of seventeen so that I could live without having to worry constantly about the needs of everyone around me. I created a bubble of cheap lifestyle, low expectations, and compulsive research of my own interests for nearly a decade. I was thoroughly insulated from the realization that my goals, needs, and desires were different from everyone else's. Until I wasn't. Until at nearly thirty, I had no car, a master's degree but no job, and a broken hand.

I'm Michael. I'm Queer, gender variant, and mid-transition. I've written multiple books and seen my essays and poetry published in several venues, I've opened and folded several businesses, never worked a full-time job, and also never worked less than fifty hours a week between my scholarship and my wage labor. I have reached sensory regulation through pain management, including kink, and I am as far from the asexual Autistic stereotype as you can get. I also have a hard time establishing trust because of my past, and while I might not always track your intentions because your face moves in more ways than you think it does, I'm getting better all the time at finding the ways to judge authenticity through action instead of social overture. I don't know how to cope with the sounds of traffic, but I also don't understand sometimes that writing over a hundred pages a week is hard for people. I try, though, because I want those same people to understand why grocery stores are hell on earth for me, and why not wanting to be seen in public doesn't mean I don't like people.

I'm *that* autistic. And I'm sick of other people telling me that I'm not.

We need more voices.

❖ ❖ ❖

Elizabeth J. (Ibby) Grace

Elizabeth J. (Ibby) Grace is a usually-speaking Autistic activist and Assistant Professor of Education at National Louis University in Chicago, where she lives in the suburbs with her family. She blogs at tinygracenotes.blogspot.com and is an editor on i.e.: inquiry in education *(digitalcommons.nl.edu/ie/) and* NeuroQueer *(neuroqueer.blogspot.com). Her writing can also be found among other places in the books* Loud Hands, Both Sides of the Table: Autoethnographies of Educators Learning and Teaching With/In [Dis]ability, *and* Criptiques. *Ibby currently serves on the board of directors of the Society for Disability Studies.*

Ibby is one of the people I am most grateful for in the Autistic community. It was Ibby who took me under her wing for a while and spoke to me about what true acceptance of Autistic kids looks like. It is because of Ibby that I met most of the other people who contributed to this book; she introduced me to them and vouched for me when I was the "new parent on the block." She believed in me. She also answered a lot of my questions about activism and advocacy.

Ibby has an amazing blog called *Tiny Grace Notes*, which I love because in it she answers questions and answering questions is something Ibby is very good at. Ibby has a way of writing that feels like conversation, and an outlook on life that I find refreshing and encouraging.

The first thing from Ibby I am sharing with you is about stimming, in a round-about way, but it is mostly about acceptance. It is called "I Am a Mother." It was written in 2012, but I only saw it recently. It shows Ibby's heart, and is a wonderful example of parents supporting each other and their children.

The second article from Ibby was published on a group blog called *We Are Like Your Child*[1]. It is a candid exposé of what it is like for Ibby, as an Autistic person, to navigate social stuff. I have included it here because it provides invaluable insight for non-Autistic parents into the challenges their children face, at the same time providing solutions that may work for them as well. I find Ibby's writing in this article to be particularly helpful in supporting my Autistic son, who is a teen fast approaching adulthood.

---

1.   URL: http://wearelikeyourchild.blogspot.com.au

I am a Mother

Elizabeth J. Grace

Layenie, my wife, is a pediatric nurse. In the US, RNs (registered nurses) are trained to be proficient at all kinds of nursing and prepared for whatever comes up. In the UK, where she was first educated in the nursing profession, candidates must choose a field of specialization, and Layenie chose pediatrics. Consequently I feel very comfortable asking her questions about the health and development of our young sons. They will turn one in January and ahhh they are soooo adorable.

It was the other evening, and I had been staying home with the boys, which I do once a week, because, you know, childcare costs a lot, and also, as I said, adorable. Benjy was doing this thing with his hand which is very like something I also do with my own hand, so this is what I said, and although I am not usually able to hear myself, I can derive a proper quote from the ensuing conversation:

Ib: "See what Benjy's doing with his hand there…. Is that OK?"

Layenie: "Yes, he's learning to wave, which is developmentally—wait. Wait a minute. Of course it's OK. Even if he's doing it just for fun or because it feels good, it's going to be OK, OK? You do things like that, and you're OK. Does it ruin your life?"

Ib: "Well…" (I was thinking about the past, about the hard things, about the things I didn't want my boy to have to live through, like school, if he is like me.)

Layenie: (As if she could hear the inside of my head, rapidly changing the scenery—) "How 'bout now? Does it ruin your life now?"

Ib: (Contemplating the Now, beaming, andd…. there goes my flappy hand) "No. My life is awesome."

Layenie: "I love your hands and I love you." (This made me cry tears of joy, and made me think.)

Then she carried on doing what she was doing with the kids but I went inside my own head a bit and crawled all over myself: hypocrite much? Would I have wanted to silence Benjy's hands? No. I am not a hypocrite, I just wanted to help him gird his loins, if necessary, for the slings and arrows of—but then I thought about it some more—a world that is largely not the same as it was. The world is better now. It really actually is, and it is moving in the right direction.

Not that it is easy now. Now, we are called burdens and a crisis and a national epidemic. Horrible "schools" still need to be closed and children are being killed to this day as a result of the way we are portrayed. But people are starting to protest this, people's mothers are starting to notice and say Hey: stop talking about my baby like that, I'm talking to you, stop it right now. And they are going to have to listen. And we are saying it and we are typing it and we are even getting into Washington DC and on TV and saying Hey: stop talking about us like that, I'm talking to you, stop it right now. And they are going to have to listen. And things will change even more. Autistics and our families TOGETHER.

When I was in school, we were called nothing, we were nowhere, we were hidden in institutions, a mystery, something to be very afraid of. Violent, "idiot savants" (I have actually been called "idiot savant" to my face in front of a room full of people), and "morons," and "mentally retarded with autistic features" (I am sorry for the language but I have read so much of this language in the historical files of my friends). Any "refrigerator mother" who was defiant or foolish enough to keep us out of institutions deserved what she got and there weren't enough of those to get us on protected lists or legal classifications or parent-to-parent support networks. Our mothers, forever considered at fault, had no way to find each other, and every reason to hide themselves in shame trying to rebuild their lives, since most of them would never see their children again. For those who kept their children against all odds, they needed support even more, but where to find it? Probably we would become homelessness statistics and end up in jails if we could talk. And if we couldn't, the protection people would put us in institutions anyway and arrest the alleged "refrigerator mothers" who had tried to keep us out, if they were poor, or make them poor, if they had financial means.

The world changes slowly, but it changes, and I am celebrating that, today. If Benjy does his hands like that because he is stimming, if JoJo rocks because he rocks like I rock, may the world keep moving into the world I want it to be for him. May I be tireless in helping to see this happen.

I am a mother. I know what the depth of this prayer feels like.

Thanks for listening, and thanks to all who pray and enact it with me.

Ib

Socio-Sensory Distress is Harsh, but Navigable
Elizabeth J. Grace

Trigger warning: Graphic descriptions of anxiety and pain and wishing to be not-me.

Disclaimer: I speak for myself, but publicly, in case others (maybe kids) may relate.

Up all night thinking about these things, unable to sleep guts twisting as if moved by the spokes of a dullish grappling hook churning slowly round, roiling the inevitable acidic bile I could not determine whether or not would come up if I tried to vomit. It's not that easy; it's not that easy to tell: it's not up to me. However familiar, the nausea has never accepted me as sovereign.

Being sociable has never really been a matter of just do it, get over it, hoist your bootstraps, yar yar yar. Some people think it is, and I can tell that this is what they think (it is very easy to tell when they proclaim such aphorisms) and I bought it early on in my life, and it made me want to wake up not-me, and give myself more grief than ever they could. I knew I was weak, even craven. I didn't ever need them to tell me so often, in so many ways, so many clichés.

Here is what a social event may be like: there is nowhere to go. And everywhere noise, and smells, noise, visual and audio noise, noise for all the senses, noise and information. And the sense data are far too many, and there are also emotional data that come flying at you from so many directions, and the atmosphere so thick you cannot breathe, even if you had been otherwise able to have a slim chance at breathing despite the light fixtures, invariably tuned to some kind of painful. And all the people are wanting, they need and want from you all the things in the wide array, and you can feel it, and what they say is not the same as what they show. There is no comfort anchor anywhere, and no dictionary of them.

All the people are talking at the same time and there are secret reasons to know to whom you are supposed to be listening more, and what you are allowed to say. The secret was not given to you, and you do not know where to find it. Meanwhile the couple to whom you were just introduced by an alpha person and (at least this time you know one thing) this means your attention is required, these people just as one example are telling you how much they love each other and are happy to meet you, while flinging emo-data of hostility toward you and belligerence to one another, hard. Your teeth hurt. You must listen because you know this rule, but all the people in this world are also simultaneously talking, very loudly, and you can only really pick up every third inconsistent lie-sounding word, and your heart bleeds for them, and there is nothing you can do, because which is stronger, your bleeding heart or your drastic incapacity? Will your heart bleed out?

You concentrate, with all you have, and your head throbs, and the knives of light stab your eye through into your brain because the dreaded cluster headache is coming which may knock you out. (It never does completely. It is too cruel for that.) You can barely hear and you try to control your face the friendly way, desperate to show your caring in a composition in which it will be correctly read. You hear someone you respect say this: "You're not present; you're not with us." Shades of "your own little world," and though you hurt to hear it, in all honesty you'd give anything, anything, for your alleged stereotypical own little world right now but you have risked it all to be in this world, this world of pain and fear and angst and constant assault and never knowing what to do or if it is right because you love the people and you want to be...

I'll say it. I will. I will say it: You want to be a person.

And now I shall just easily bootstrap over my just do it and finish writing this.

These things are always worse for me beforehand, in the imagining, especially when someone has been sort of mean or unwelcoming in the lead-up and I have let it spin out of control inside my head. In real life, I have ways of working with it, and I will write some of them here, because in real life, I get through, and often come out the other end very, very tired, sure, but saying it was fun.

Because of this: usually it was the case that I had fun. I do love other people and in reality believe I am a person.

I am, you know, a person.

A while ago some things happened. One of which was this. I found out it hurts people's feelings when you never come to their parties. So I wanted to find a workaround. Then soon thereafter I found out that in order to have a professional life you have to do certain kinds of social events whether people's feelings get hurt or not, because that is the way of the world. So I needed to find several workarounds.

One of the first things I do when I can is case the joint. I try to find the lay of the land. This gives me a modicum of physical comfort. Also this leads into the second strategy I have, which is one of my most potent go-to items: giving myself secret jobs. For example, inside my head, I may be The One Who Is Secretly In Charge Of Replenishing Drinks. Or The One Who Knows Where All The People Are, In Case Anyone Should Ask. This is very diverting, and gives me a sense of belonging. Also, it causes me to act in ways that transmit my role to those around me, thereby making their actions toward me more predictable and easy to read. Ahhh… comfort.

My mother came up with a good overall strategy once I started needing a more advanced go-to, one for situations and events in which I had not had a chance to case the joint and invent a role. It goes like this, and it has worked well for me. My role in the event is to scan the environment for someone(s) who appears to feel even more uncomfortable or out of place than I feel inside, and show them welcome and a good time. This is more advanced than the strategies above because it does take a certain amount of practice and core confidence to pull this off; for example, I cannot do it while in mid-meltdown. Sometimes when I am particularly ill-at-ease in a given situation I will start out being The Drink Replenisher and that will relax me enough to allow me to become The Noticing Welcomer.

What is great about it when I am able to relax enough to become the person who can see that there are others who are even more crushed and stabbed and roiling in the anxiety blender than I am, is that not only am I distracted from the overreactions of my own body, but I am useful, and that makes my body calm down, because it is a good job. And my calm body can bring calm to the bodies of others because that is how things work in the world. I know I can make things less difficult because I know that I do understand what it is, and I will never say oh, bootstraps chin up just do it yar yar. I will say I see you, and I welcome you.

And in so doing, I welcome a person, and bestow upon myself the right to offer welcome.

I have recognized the personhood of both of us.

Later, I will be very, very tired, but I may have made a new friend, and I will be happy.

These things take practice, and the willingness to risk, but they have been worth it in my life.

Thank you for listening,

Love,

Ib

Briannon Lee

Briannon is a queer autistic woman living in Brisbane, Australia with her partner, Jules, and their three children. A social worker by trade with a passion for social justice, Briannon also has a background in biomedical science. After a decade of researching and writing about policy and service delivery issues relating to vulnerable people, she has recently started writing about issues closer to home and heart, such as parenting and autistic rights. She currently contributes to the group blogging project Respectfully Connected[1].

Briannon wrote this piece specifically for this book. When I first read it I felt honoured that she has shared such a personal part of her story with us.

Understanding intersectionality (intersections between forms or systems of oppression or discrimination) and the implications of it in our lives is important. It is quite common for Autistic people to find themselves in more than one minority group. This is something Briannon talks about with experience as a queer autistic woman. Any family like mine, where multiple diagnoses exist, will also experience oppression and discrimination in multiple ways, so this has been an important subject for me to explore. Briannon's vulnerability provides a degree of insight not often offered, and helps me understand the need for my children to always have a safe place to return to.

In many ways this piece is confronting. It reminds me of the othering my kids face and how important it is for me to advocate for their needs over my own desires. It reminds me that it is always hard work for them, even when they appear to be coping well. As parents

---

1.   URL: http://respectfullyconnected.blogspot.com.au

we all want what is best for our children. In this piece Briannon beautifully expresses what that means for her as an Autistic mother. It is insight that all parents of Autistic children will find valuable.

Finding Querencia

Briannon Lee

I am a Chameleon. By nature and necessity.
Right now, I live among You. In Your community.
We are white, cisgender, middle class families. We live a privileged, suburban existence.

But I am not You, despite Your protests and assurances, attempts at assimilation.

I am a lesbian, Autistic woman.
We are a two mummy family.
We are neurodivergent.
Three children, gay babies, conceived with donor sperm. Fatherless by our choice. Twins, born prematurely. We have anxiety, a rare chromosome disorder, speech and motor delays.

We have no place in Your community.

We have no place in Your heterosexual mothers groups, and suburban playgrounds, where we are at best, Your new age friends or a tool for Your education. At worst, we are blamed for our children's actions, for their disabilities.

We have no place, in Your Queer community with Your shiny Rainbow Families, where we are misunderstood. We are too different. Hard to accommodate. A minority within.

We have no place in Your 'Special Needs' community, with Your Autism mums and dads whose identity is caught up in grief and sacrifice. We are too Autistic for you. Too happy for you. Too Queer for you.

Before parenthood, I always somehow found a small place of belonging within the community I was living in. But now, as a mother raising my children in Your suburban community, there is no place for us.

So I have created my own place. I call it Querencia.

Defined in the Oxford Dictionary, "Spanish, literally 'lair, home ground,' from querer 'desire, love,' from Latin quaerere 'seek.'"

Querencia. The place that I seek, that I desire. Love. My home ground, my lair.

Querencia. A gift passed to me from my parents, who determinedly shaped a safe and loving home for their family; where four children grew to be adults, were free to leave and always welcome to return.

When I did not return, it was because I found my Querencia in the arms of a woman who grounded me like no other. My Querencia is built on our love. It has grown stronger over the years. The birth of our children, sickness, death, and betrayals, have left our Querencia weathered but beautiful, now stretching up to the sky, allowing only the loveliest, most unique creatures to come and join us within.

Our Querencia is the place I yearn to be as soon as I leave; it is the only place that I can truly be myself. That sweet place where I can take refuge and regain my strength. It is my lair, where my children are protected and nurtured. We thrive here, amongst You, but away from You.

The word querencia is frequently applied to bullfighting, as the place of safety that the bull will return to in the Arena, to reclaim its strength and power.

And indeed, Your world is my bullring. I am the bull, free, proud and strong. You the Matador.

Imagine,

I venture out to Your suburban shopping centre with my children. Smells and sounds encroach on my brain. Your perfume, Your music,

Your lights. Words, everywhere, asking to be read. Too many details to absorb.

My brain is screaming, my children squealing. And while we are there, my family, trying to buy bread, I meet You. Matador.

You say,

You've got your hands full!
Does he always make those noises?
I'm so sorry to hear he's on the spectrum.
Special kids go to special people.
Is your husband a bit Aspie?
But then, who is the real mother?
How did you decide who would have the babies?
Yes, but where is their father? Children need fathers.
Did you pick sperm out of a catalogue?
Is the donor Autistic?
Does he know about your children's problems?
I used to work with a little Autistic boy, he was really cute, like Rain Man.
You can't be Autistic. You don't look Autistic. Not even Aspie.
We're all on the spectrum somewhere.
What do you think about gay marriage?
Are you sure she's autistic? She just made a lot of eye contact with me.
I really do think we are too quick to label and categorise children these days. All children are unique.
I hope to bump in to you again sometime soon, it was lovely to chat.

It is said that a bull trying to reach its querencia is more dangerous than a bull that is attacking the cape directly.

In these moments with You, all I can think of is returning myself and my babies to our Querencia. I will do anything to get there as fast as possible. Sometimes that means engaging in conversation with You. I do not engage for Your sake, for Your education. I do not want to share intimate details of my family life with a stranger. I comply only to escape. My eyes are set on Querencia.

Sometimes in these moments with You, I am dangerous like the bull. I don't want any of Your ignorance, thinly-veiled in pleasantries. I only want to reach my Querencia, and You are in my way. I practice my responses at night, so that they slip off the tongue perfectly. I wield my words as weapons. I speak loudly so others hear.

So that my children hear.

They are in the bullring already. You talk about them in their presence. Some days You talk directly to them. They are exposed to Your thoughts about them in the media and online, where gay marriage debates and autism epidemics and cures are hot topics. Their lives are Your hot topics.

They will be adults one day. They might choose, as I have, to live among You.

I hope they can be free, proud and strong like the bull.
I hope they can wield their words and actions to defend and attack.

I hope they can find their Querencia, as my parents did, and as I have. The place that they seek, desire and love. Their lair. An environment that soothes. A place where they can be nurtured, regain their strength, and experience unconditional love and acceptance.

This is my wish too, for all my fellow Chameleons, for all those who are too different, whose identities intersect to push them out further on the margins, who feel like freak shows or educational tools for the uninformed privileged masses, who get asked too many questions, who feel like they are constantly in the Bullring; may they find their Querencia too.

And while we walk among You, I beg of You, leave us to be free, proud and strong.

❖ ❖ ❖

Morénike Giwa Onaiwu

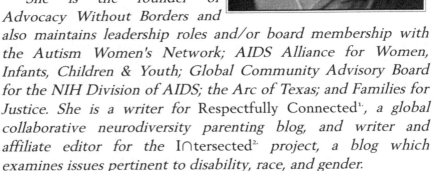

Morénike Giwa Onaiwu is a mom, community advocate, and writer. An Autistic woman of color in a multicultural, neurodivergent, HIV-affected family, Morénike is heavily involved in various social justice activism endeavors including HIV-related advocacy, disability rights, research, gender and racial justice, and promoting acceptance, inclusion, and neurodiversity.

She is the founder of Advocacy Without Borders and also maintains leadership roles and/or board membership with the Autism Women's Network; AIDS Alliance for Women, Infants, Children & Youth; Global Community Advisory Board for the NIH Division of AIDS; the Arc of Texas; and Families for Justice. She is a writer for Respectfully Connected[1]*, a global collaborative neurodiversity parenting blog, and writer and affiliate editor for the* I∩tersected[2] *project, a blog which examines issues pertinent to disability, race, and gender.*

Additionally, she is affiliated with several other community groups as an active member, and also engages regularly in online and social media advocacy campaigns and projects. When not online, she volunteers, writes, and presents at state and national research, advocacy, and disability conferences.

Morénike, who loves travel, reading, music, and Thai food, considers herself a Christian humanist and a "life-long learner" who is constantly growing and changing, hopefully for the better! She considers her six children, ranging from pre-K to college and

---

1.   URL: http://respectfullyconnected.blogspot.com/
2.   URL: http://intersecteddisability.blogspot.com/

both biological and adopted, to be her greatest accomplishment.

I met Morénike only recently through an advocacy group we both contribute to. I was immediately impressed by her transparency and her passion. As a woman who is part of numerous minority groups, Morénike's voice is one that addresses intersectionality and is vitally important to listen to. You can plainly see Morénike's heart for justice when you visit her blog[1].

I've included this article of Morénike's not because it speaks about something specific to parenting young children, but because it addresses assumptions and generalisations about communication, socialising, and relationships that need to be challenged by anyone who supports an Autistic person.

---

1.   URL: http://whoneedsnormalcy.blogspot.com.au

Why I Don't Like All of Those "Get Off Social Media and Into the Real World" Posts

Morénike Giwa Onaiwu

By now we've all seen them. The videos, articles, posts, etc., that declare how "fake" social media is and stating how important it is to interact with "real people" in the "real world."

I'm not saying there isn't some merit to some of what they are saying. When possible and desired, it can be very rewarding to have face-to-face interactions with people. I'm not saying that social media should totally replace hanging out with people nor am I denying that sometimes it can be refreshing to take social media breaks or reduce the amount of time one is online.

But I am saying that these types of articles are written from a very biased, very neuro-typical point of view, and what they are implying about some of us is quite ableist and quite unfair.

Lemme break it down for y'all a bit.

Cue the 80's and 90's music. Before social media there was a little brown girl. As no teacher seemed to be able to pronounce "Morénike," she was known widely as "Nikky" (which all my old friends still call me, which is totally cool). Even as a little girl, she was better at writing than speaking. She got in trouble quite a lot from elementary school up through high school because she would write and pass notes to friends. The note-passing was not to be insubordinate, but was her only true way of getting her real thoughts out. The thoughts that didn't come freely when she was speaking because speaking was so much mental effort, even though everyone considered her a pretty good orator, especially when it came to debate. Her best ideas always came when she had a pen and paper in her hand. The same was true for academics, not just social interactions; her written reports were always far better than her oral reports. An undiagnosed autistic who was also hyperlexic and gifted, especially in verbal reasoning, she considered, and sometimes stated, that writing was her true "first language."

She didn't hate "being with people." She actually loved people. But it wasn't easy. She was both introverted and very social at the same time. No one knew the secret inner panic she felt about crowds, or parties, or groups of people. She hid it well. But sometimes it still came out, both in childhood/adolescence and in adulthood. In her late teens and early twenties, for example, it was not uncommon after a night at the club with friends (and/or after hours of socializing in big crowds) for her to become emotional, get into a disagreement with someone over something seemingly trivial in the car on the way home, and literally jump out of the vehicle and attempt to walk home. Her friends didn't understand these outbursts, though they tried to support her through them. She didn't understand them either. But she knew that she felt "caged" and that getting out of the car and walking was the only way she knew to regain control, to clear her mind, to get some breathing space away from everyone. Even though these were the people she loved best in the world, it was too much sometimes.

Might sound odd, but it was—is—me. Fast-forward lots of years ahead, and there are many such scenarios like that. Perhaps not as dramatic as exiting a vehicle at three in the morning and trying to walk home in high heels and short shorts in the dark, but the same theme emerges. Requesting and paying extra for a single room in college to have some space. Working through lunch breaks at work to avoid having to socialize with co-workers. Declining the invitation to a party or other outing out of fatigue. Etc, etc. Not really conscious of how or why at the time, I've always needed to build in "space" and "breaks" for myself to be able to function. Socializing takes a lot out of me. I enjoy it, but I have to be prepared before it, and I have to be able to "come down" after it.

But not all social interaction is built equally. I don't feel the same, nor act the same, in all settings. My special interests are learning, advocacy, and social justice, and I shine in social interactions where those areas are involved. Whether having a one-on-one conversation or presenting on a stage in front of a crowd of hundreds, once I get past the first few moments of jitters, I'm totally cool. I'm in my zone when I'm talking about and doing things that I am passionate about. When I am advocating and educating, the social anxiety can't reach me because I'm much too high. In those moments, my "deficits"— perseveration, intense focus, preoccupation with details, verbosity, atypical prosody, heightened sense of feeling and memory, etc.—in those moments, those things aren't weaknesses. They're strengths; they're gifts. They're me. And they're freakin' beautiful, and real, and right.

However, this same woman (me), who can speak effectively and without fear in front of the world's leading researchers, or in front of government officials, or in front of celebrities... this same woman has to spend fifteen minutes in the car praying and doing deep breathing before volunteering at my children's schools (oh, the small talk!) or before calling up an old friend (texting is so much nicer), etc. These are people I like, and yet it's hard for me. It is exponentially harder in forced interactions with people I don't know or don't like.

With writing, though, none of this applies. I'm so free. This whole post, for example, would have been very hard to convey if I had to "tell" it to you aloud. When my fingers are on a keyboard, or screen, or writing utensil, the real me emerges so readily. I'm free. Not that the "me" that is there when I'm in person isn't real; it is. But less certain, less meaningfully communicative, less... me. Kind of like a person speaking a foreign language. You can live in a country for 20 years and the language of that land is now very familiar to you. You now speak that language quite well, but it will never come with the ease and natural comfort of your native tongue. In your second language you might be "good," but in your native tongue you are almost great.

However, social interaction is a part of life, and cannot be entirely avoided (nor should it be). Those of us who aren't the best at it still have to engage in it. And I have done so for years, and did okay. Some years better than others, but still sorta okay. But then something happened that changed the dynamic quite a bit. If it was a book title, I'd call it "Six Kids in Six Years: The Accidental Family." My family has grown exponentially in a short period of time, and it was the best "accident" I could have ever been blessed with. Once, in what seems almost like another life, I was facing the prospect of not knowing if I'd ever be able to be a parent; now my "cup runneth over." I have a large, loud, loving, neurodiverse family, and I wouldn't have it any other way. They are my world, and they have my heart.

But.

They have needs. A lot of them. They need support. Encouragement. Nurturing. Guidance. Care. Love. They need a lot from me, and I am here to give it. But that means I don't have a lot of me left for other people sometimes. Not in a bad way; I care deeply for others, and try my best to be there for them. But my family comes first, last, and always before anyone and anything. Kid gets sick on the night of my high school reunion? Y'all have fun; I'm staying home. AIDS Walk falls during an important international conference? I'm leaving the conference; flying home early to walk with my people. Got an invite to a cool concert, but my kid starts having meltdowns/panic attacks/seizures before I'm supposed to leave? I ask another friend to go in my place. I don't mean for it to be the case, but life happens... and when you have a family as big as mine, life happens a lot. And without regret or hesitation, when life happens to my family I know exactly where I want to be and where I choose to be: with my family.

And then sometimes life doesn't happen. There are days that things are pretty calm (our version of calm, anyway). When things aren't super busy and nothing chaotic or catastrophic is going on. A lot of days are happy, and fun, and filled with memories. Thank God, more days are good than bad. But even on those days, my emotional capacity, my mental and physical energy, my socializing quota... all of those things are finite even on my best day. And you might find that even on the days when the sky is not falling and my face has been full of smiles, I still may not be able to socialize face-to-face. Because on good days I still have to drive four hours or more roundtrip getting the kids to and from school; I still might have to host a conference call; I still likely have to deal with things that require some of my "spoons." So even on a good day, when that phone call is coming in I might (not even "might"—probably "will") have to let it go to voicemail (which I almost never check). On a good day I still might have to let a little time go by before I check emails or texts. Because I just may not be able to handle communication at that moment... just because. I have a limited amount of energy to expend each day, and most of it is going to be reserved for my family. Whatever I have left is for everyone and everything else.

So... that doesn't exactly make for a hopping social life in the "real world." In fact, about a month or so after my sons first joined our family a few years ago, one of them asked me, "Mom, do you have friends? Hardly anyone comes over here." Lol!

Then something pretty incredible happened. Three something incredibles even.

My available time for socializing and advocating increased because my children all went to school (even the little ones, thanks to the public preschool for children with disabilities, which enrolls eligible children as young as three years old).

We switched to a cell phone plan with a HUGE amount of data.

One of my very good friends sweetly convinced me to get with the 21st century and give social media, which I had been purposely avoiding for years, a try.

And life changed.

My advocacy efforts expanded, because now I didn't have to do so much of it face to face. I gained access to a lot of exciting information and opportunities, and people. And I got a chance to socialize online instead of solely in person. I found that socializing, which was once a challenge, became practically painless. Now it was controlled, safe, and not tied to knowing when to look up, how loud or soft to make one's voice, when to laugh and when not to, when to gesture and when not to, whether or not to make eye contact, whether I was stimming or hiding it, etc. And when I was getting overstimulated, or if I needed to go do something or attend to something or someone? I just logged off and went to take care of my business; no worries. It. Was. Awesome!

I found that my in-person socializing actually improved as well, because now I was less stressed out about it. My life in general became a lot less stressful.

I have met amazing people who I care for deeply on this "fake" social media. People I'd fight for. People who are fighting for me. People I will happily support if they need me, and who are doing the same for me. People I would have likely never met "IRL" (in "real life") for various reasons. And this same "fake" social media has allowed me to see a different side of people that I *do* know in person, and has often helped me to actually like them more and feel like I can better interact with them socially in person as a result of our interactions online.

I admit it's not all rainbows and butterflies. I've seen the drama. I've seen the bullying. I've seen the unpleasant. Just like "IRL," there is good and bad to social media. I'm not pretending it's all wonderful.

But just because there are some bad elements of something, that doesn't make it altogether bad. Or fake. Or weird. I am *myself* online. I don't create a fake persona of someone who is perfect or gorgeous or rich or super-important. I'm just me.

All of those "be with *real* people; get offline" posts are insulting. I *am* a real person. For various reasons, being with "real" people in person frequently is not possible or desirable for me. Being online gives me access to people and places that are difficult for me to navigate. To insinuate that people like me are shallow, fake, or depriving ourselves because our preferred mode of socialization differs from others is unfair.

I socialize more easily this way because I am autistic, I am busy, I am a mom with a large family of which many members have disabilities and require extensive time and support, and socializing online is less stress-inducing. Some people socialize better online because they have geographic constraints, because of physical/mental/emotional disability, and/or for other reasons.

We respect people's right to small talk, to being around people all the time, and to socializing the way that works best for them. Please respect the right of people like me to socialize the way that works best for us.

Thanks bunches for understanding. See ya on Twitter!

Amy Sequenzia

Amy Sequenzia is a multiply-disabled, non-speaking Autistic activist and writer. Amy writes about disability rights, civil rights, and human rights. She also writes poetry.

Amy has presented in several conferences in the US and abroad, and her work is featured in books about being Autistic and Disabled. Amy is deeply involved with the Neurodiversity Movement and has been outspoken about the rights and worth of disabled people.

Amy serves on the Board of Directors of the Autistic Self Advocacy Network (ASAN), the Autism National Committee (AutCom), and the Florida Alliance for Assistive Services and Technology (FAAST).

Amy blogs for Autism Women's Network and for the disability rights and resources website Ollibean[1]*. She also guest-blogs for several other websites. All her online published work can be found on her own blog,* Non-Speaking Autistic Speaking[2]*.*

Although it's a bit embarrassing, I will admit I was a bit "star-struck" when I first met Amy online. I had been reading her work for quite a while and had developed a lot of respect for her.

Amy's blog, *Non-Speaking Autistic Speaking*, is an absolute must-read for all parents of Autistic children. As a non-speaking Autistic adult her voice in the conversation about supporting Autistic children is invaluable. Her advocacy and activism flies in the face of the myth that non-speaking kids have less capacity to understand and communicate their likes, dislikes, needs, thoughts, and wishes.

Aside from that, Amy is a stellar human being whose passion to see

1. URL: http://ollibean.com/
2. URL: http://nonspeakingautisticspeaking.blogspot.com

all people treated fairly stands out as an example to the many who admire her thoughtful and wise words. I am grateful for her work advocating for the Autistic community, and thankful she goes before my kids in the fight for the rights of all disabled people to be heard in conversations about their needs.

This series of posts on common attitudes about autism and disability, which Amy has generously agreed to have published here in its entirety, was first published on ollibean.com. Unfortunately, in print form Amy's writing loses some of its richness and complexity, as the links to previous articles and other relevant background are lost. If you are the kind of person who revels in knowing the whole story and seeing the full picture, a visit to the Ollibean website to see this series in its original form is well worth your time.

Attitudes – Introduction

Amy Sequenzia

When you are disabled there is a lot going against you. Not that disability is the worst thing someone can experience. It is not. Disability can be hard and some things can be very difficult to deal with. Some of us need medication and managing this can be difficult; some of us experience pain and this can be energy draining; others might have trouble with sensory processing; some might even need hospitalization from time to time.

Different disabilities require different approaches, and different types of accommodations. What non-disabled people should remember is that we either learn how to live as a disabled person, if the disability is a result of an illness or injury, or we just live our lives the way we know how, because when you are born disabled it is not possible for you to "miss" being non-disabled. We only know ourselves as we are.

But one of the most difficult things a person with a disability has to deal with, and this happens all the time, is the attitude of non-disabled people.

Here is why:

In general, people look at us and feel pity and sorrow because we are disabled. They cannot see us as human beings, with human feelings, human goals, human desires, human qualities. We are seen only as people who need to be taken care of, instead of human beings who need help to achieve some of the same goals non-disabled people have. There is an assumption that we are suffering and that our lives are not really fulfilling. This can lead to a lack of interest in investing in us, in giving us equal rights and accommodating our needs.

Everybody needs help with one thing or another, but disabled people usually need help throughout their lives. Somehow "help" became associated with "shame."

"Help" is also associated with "burden" and we are often blamed for things we cannot control.

Society, through its attitude toward us, resents our existence.

When we want to participate in everyday decisions, when we decide that we do not want to be patronized, when we speak up and show disagreement with people who are also our "helpers," our competency is often questioned and our wishes ignored.

Being disabled is not usually associated with self-determination, and we are often seen as the ones who should be loudly grateful for what others "do for us," while being silently compliant, even if we don't agree with what non-disabled people say is "best" for us.

Pity. Resentment. Incompetence.

Those attitudes devalue us. More than any difficulties or complications caused by our disabilities, the perceptions propagated by such attitudes create a false assumption that we suffer and that we should not have too many goals or hopes, that we do not have worth, that whatever little support, accommodation, attention and participation we receive, we should accept and keep silent.

We should not complain, demand, try to participate and be included. "Disability is a natural part of the human experience", says the ADA. In practice, though, disabled people are seen as an economic burden, while our social value is ignored.

We are also seen as a burden to service providers and institutions, like schools and work places. Accommodations needed for our full participation are seen as something that will cost time, money, resources, and the effort of a new way of thinking.

A new way of thinking. This is the way to go.

Our culture is ingrained with wrong assumptions, misinformation, lack of understanding, and unwillingness to change all that.

We need to start to change how non-disabled people see disabled people, and then we can begin demanding a change in attitude. It is not an easy task but we are growing, not only in numbers, but also in self-awareness, self-determination and pride.

Let's not wait for the non-disabled to offer us what they want to offer for our success. The definition of success should come from each one of us, according to what we want for our own lives. We have enough true allies to join and support us, and we can demand what we decide we need to live a fulfilling human life.

❖ ❖ ❖

Attitudes – Communication

Amy Sequenzia

Communication is not only speaking, typing, texting, or signing.

Communication is also being able to listen and understand, being accommodated to make interaction possible.

(Thank you Henry Frost for the input on implants, hearing aids and how Deaf students need more accessibility)

I wrote about how attitudes toward disabled people[3] can help or hamper us. I want to talk about attitudes in communication, or how non-disabled people need to understand a few things.

First thing, everybody communicates.

I will say it again: everybody communicates.

If you don't understand the method, this only means that you don't understand, not that there is no communication.

Disabled people who have difficulties with expressive language, or who are non-speaking, are often thought of as not being able to communicate. This is because the majority is sometimes too lazy to think outside the box. Yes, I said lazy. We also find it hard to understand the majority's language but we are pushed and forced to learn it, and to act in compliance with the majority's way of doing things. Even when we are only a few steps from the majority's way, it is never good enough. We are consider to be "able to communicate" only if we speak, and act in accordance with, the language the majority chooses to know.

This attitude, seen in parents, teachers, and other professionals, is one of the things that need to change.

I am a non-speaking Autistic who has learnt how to communicate in a way that the majority is able to understand. It was not easy, it still isn't. Even after I had shown how much I knew, how much I was learning, despite not being formally taught, even if I no longer cried as a way to let people know that I was trying to convey a message[4], the default attitude of teachers, doctors and others was still dismissive. The attitude of the groups I mentioned are still dismissive. I believe this is

3.   See "Attitudes – Introduction", p. 86.
4.   Endow, J. (2013, Aug 20). "We are Not in Our Own World." ***Ollibean.com*** URL:
     http://ollibean.com/2013/08/20/world/

also true for other disabled people who don't communicate in what is considered "the normal way".

The damaging attitudes toward different methods of communication hurt us not only when we want to be heard, but also when we want to participate or be social, or when we want to listen.

Attitudes toward communication reflect the big problem of non-disabled people regarding disabilities: there is too much "awareness" but too little understanding.

Even the Deaf community, which has been so loud for a long time, and has seen its rights to use its own language more broadly accepted, still faces obstacles when captions and interpreters are not offered as a matter of course.

Deaf children in schools have to fight to keep up with the content of lessons if they are expected to access the instruction without the accommodations they need. Without access to captions, interpreters, or note takers, they do not receive the same information about the lesson as their classmates.

It doesn't seem to be better if a Deaf person has a cochlear implant or hearing aids. There is a false belief that the implant "cures" deafness, when the truth is that the ones with an aid or implant still need accommodations to fully participate: many words are hard to understand and environmental noises are amplified.

Communication is not only speaking, through speech, signs, text, or typing. Gestures, eye movement, body language, or any sound, are also forms of communication.

Communication is also listening and interacting, allowing the necessary time for the interaction to happen.

As someone who types and who can have conversations using my AAC device, I often experience what I call a "bad attitude" from the ones interacting with me: many don't wait for me to finish my typing, they get impatient.

Typing is not just strokes on a keyboard. It takes us a lot of effort to make the command given by the brain travel to the hands and fingers and hit the right letter. The process does not get easier as we type letters and words. It is still the same hard work, letter after letter, word after word, sentence after sentence. And most of us use only one finger to type, which makes the whole process even slower.

Besides the extra time required, we might also need breaks from time to time, we might need to walk a little, move, flap, or jump. Those things help us relieve the anxiety, they help us recharge the brain for more work. Those things are part of how we communicate. If you want to understand us, to interact with us, you need to know that, respect that.

Attitudes about disabled people who communicate differently need to change on many levels.

We need time to process the information and to express our thoughts.

We need access to captions, devices, interpreters, and facilitators.

We need access to a proper environment where we can truly communicate, meaning being heard and being able to listen and to understand.

We need to be not only respected, but also included. This means being part of conferences, boards of directors, opinion pieces, plays, and TV shows, where our chosen method of communication is fully embraced.

We need to be respected as fully humans because even as we prove our competence, some people still refuse to approach us, choosing instead to communicate with our support friends.

We need to be respected because the way we communicate might mean doing things and acting in ways that might not seem to be related to communication.

We, the ones outside the majority's definition of "normal and acceptable communication" have been learning your methods since ever.

It is time for the majority to take a few steps toward us and embrace our methods.

I know there have been improvements but disabled students still struggle to be included, disabled workers are not accommodated, only because their method of communication requires the majority to take a step toward them.

That is what I mean by changing attitudes regarding communication and disabilities.

It is time for the majority to learn, respect, and embrace how each one of us communicates.

❖ ❖ ❖

Attitudes – Grading People

Amy Sequenzia

Parents and family of disabled people should start demanding that everyone who is part of their children's lives stops using functioning labels. We don't need to be graded. We already have value.

Disabled people are graded. Unlike non-disabled people, our perceived value in society depends on how "comfortable" the majority feels about us. This is another way of looking at functioning labels[5].

Non-disabled people, the majority of them, prefer to accept the absurd idea that, when you are disabled, you must be categorized in one of two classes: a "low" class or a "high" class.

This kind of "acceptance" occurs because some people are too apathetic to question and defy the wrong idea that disabled people don't ever change, learn, or experience and react to events in a human way.

This is the same group of people that agrees that we must be "fixed" and "improved" in order to be "allowed" to make choices and to be heard.

It should be noted that professionals who don't give up using functioning labels are often profiting from approaches that would "make us better, more like normal people." They make money by grading disabled people and promoting approaches, which they call "therapies," that make the majority feel better about our existence.

But they are not the only ones using functioning labels, and they are not the only ones hurting us.

Let's begin with parents.

First, what I say here is not "ignore the difficulties," but rather value your children's strengths, support them, and help them find or learn the best way to deal with their individual difficulties. This includes therapies that value who they are and that work with them to make certain aspects of their lives easier to cope (without trying to change who they are), and also includes support with whatever is needed for them to achieve their own definition of independence, including self-

---

5. Sequenzia, A. (2013, Sept. 26). "More Problems With Functioning Labels." ***Ollibean.com***. URL: http://ollibean.com/2013/09/26/problems-functioning-labels/

determination.

You don't have to ignore doctors. Some disabilities do need a lot of medical attention. What you should ignore are predictions made by professionals who can only value human lives if those lives are as close as possible to what they see as acceptable and worthy.

If you believe your child is broken and too "low-functioning" to succeed, and if you fall for the false idea that a "low-functioning" human being even exists, you are hurting your child.

Self-esteem matters. Being assumed to be competent matters, even if we don't fulfill all of our parents' expectations. As we grow, we develop our own sense of worth and we start to develop our own goals and our expectations for ourselves. This is true for all human beings.

If all we hear is that we can't, that we need to improve, that our future will be not good because we are part of a "low" class of humans, we don't learn that we can expect to be valued for who we are. This attitude, coming from our own family, becomes a self-fulfilling prophecy.

The same is true for parents who like to set their children apart from other disabled people by making sure their "high functioning" status is always mentioned.

These parents usually don't allow the children to make mistakes, or to act in any manner that appears to be how they say a "lower functioning" person would act. This is an impossible expectation because everyone makes mistakes, messes up, and will have at least one big meltdown in their lifetime. The so-called "high-functioning" children learn to be compliant, or they learn how to hide their true selves, or they learn how to hide emotions (at a very high personal cost). They become young adults and adults who are afraid to ask for help, if they are taught that they don't need certain accommodations.

Parents' attitudes toward their children can influence how the rest of the world will see and treat the children. For parents of disabled children, attitudes that are not based on an arbitrary grading are even more important.

Because disabilities are largely seen as unfortunate, undesirable, and often tragic events, rather than a natural occurrence, or even an uninvited outcome that nonetheless becomes part of who we are, there is already great focus on defining and listing our perceived deficits.

After the list is done and we are "classified," the focus turns to trying to make us "blend" with the majority, or to "train" us to act in compliance with the majority's way.

This approach does not work and devalues who we are. Besides, the world misses out on getting to know our true selves, it misses on learning that there are many different ways to accomplish things, and that definitions like "success" and "independence" are abstract, unique to each individual.

I suggest that parents and close friends of disabled people stop using functioning labels and start valuing our existence as we experience it. That's not saying that we should not be exposed to learning opportunities. It means respecting our timing, choices, and way of being.

I also suggest that parents and friends of disabled people demand that school and doctors stop using functioning labels. It may not be easy but demanding respect is worth any effort (and contrary to what people might say, using functioning labels is not necessary for services).

Let us define ourselves. No disabled person uses functioning labels as part of their identity—the ones who call themselves "high-functioning" do so because they are not yet accepting of their disability, or because they are supremacists, trying to distance themselves from the "rest of us."

Respect. Attitudes need to change to allow us to function in ways that respect who we are.

Attitudes – Information and Education

Amy Sequenzia

This is especially directed at parents, family members, and all who spend a lot of time with disabled children. It also applies to adults, even if the way things happen when an adult is diagnosed or needs supports are different from how they happen with children. But we, disabled adults, also deserve to have supportive and informed people assisting us in navigating and participating in the world.

When a child is diagnosed with a disability, or born disabled, it is said that parents and family members grieve. That's probably because the general perception of any disability is a negative one. Being disabled is likened to being "trapped," "cursed," "unfortunate"; disabilities are seen as undesirable, tragic, and without hope for happiness.

It is understandable that a family that does not know much about disabilities will begin worrying before seeking the so-needed education. That's why we need a change in attitudes. Instead of listening only to doctors and "experts," seek adults with the same disability as your child —the real experts. Inform and educate yourself.

If you want to make sure your child is accepted and respected by the rest of the world, if you want your child to have opportunities, you need to connect with the ones who are like your child, even if somewhat different.

There are many proud disabled people that can give first hand information, and help families and friends by educating them about the realities of the disability.

This does not mean that things are going to be always easy and simple. It means that your child or the adult you are supporting will not be seen as someone who needs "fixing."

Disabled people are not broken, defective "almost people." Yet, the information families receive from doctors is usually a list of deficits, followed by a list of things that need fixing, plus another list of approaches that can "minimize the deficits" in the disabled child's life.

Soon after, the doctor grades the child. This needless information is delivered with a variety of tone of voice, sympathy (or lack of), frowning, and different degrees of "hope" for a "better life."

In my case, one doctor stated, sternly, that the only hope my parents should have for me was to find a "nice institution" to care for me, since I would never be able to learn anything.

One big problem is that most doctors are not educated on disabilities. To many of them, disabled equals imperfections, and they will try to "correct" those imperfections to make us look like or "function" as close to the perfect "normal" as they can.

And there is also the very real fact that many doctors and therapists make a lot of money selling treatments that will make us "better" and more "desirable." Parents are led to believe that if they don't try everything the medical establishment proposes, they are not doing all that is best for their children.

Information. Education.

Parents who want an inclusive life for their children, parents and true allies who believe every person has the right to experience life at its fullest, the way each one of us can—these parents and friends need to be informed and educated.

The best way to do that is by seeking information from other disabled people—our lives are full of happiness, sadness, ups, downs, struggles, and accomplishments, just like any other person's life.

Learn about the history of the Disability Rights Movement—facts are important if you want to fight for your child's (or an adult's) rights. History will tell you what to fight for without wasting all the energy you have. It will also help you educate others about the value of the lives of disabled people.

Seek other disabled people as role models—many of us have been through events that you would not want your child to go through, or we have learned how to be proud of who we are, and how to deal with sometimes real debilitating issues. We can help you by sharing our experience. Your child is part of our tribe and we want him to succeed.

Get involved with all the issues surrounding disabilities—it is your child's life now. Disability is not a tragedy but it is complicated sometimes. Involvement will forever be part of your life.

Keep the doctor's lists only to debunk the wrong assumptions.

Seek any therapy only after listening to several sources, than ask yourself what each therapy's goal is: to change, "fix," and teach compliance to your child, or to use the child's assets to help her be the best her she can be?

When we educate ourselves, we learn to value every achievement and every person.

Seeking members of the disability tribe is free and will teach you that "hope" is not something to long for with pain and pessimism, but a certainty that only requires respect for the human being each disabled person is.

Changing attitudes toward disabled people is an act of activism that begins with respect, information from the ones who are the only true experts, and education. This change in attitude is for your child, for the person you love, for all of us, and it can start with you.

Lightning Source UK Ltd.
Milton Keynes UK
UKOW06f2049310116

267380UK00015B/155/P